Collective Bargaining, Strikes, and Financial Costs in Public Education: A Comparative Review

Collective Bargaining, Strikes, and Financial Costs in Public Education: A Comparative Review

by
Bruce S. Cooper

with the assistance of
John C. Bussey

Foreword by
Anthony M. Cresswell

ERIC
Clearinghouse on Educational Management
University of Oregon

1982

International Standard Book Number: 0-86552-079-8
Library of Congress Catalog Card Number: 81-71248

Printed in the United States of America
ERIC Clearinghouse on Educational Management
University of Oregon, Eugene, Oregon 97403

Designed by George Beltran, University Publications, University of Oregon

This publication was prepared with funding from the National Institute of Education, U.S. Department of Education under contract no. 400-78-0007. The opinions expressed in this report do not necessarily reflect the positions or policies of NIE or the Department of Education.

About ERIC

The Educational Resources Information Center (ERIC) is a national information system operated by the National Institute of Education. ERIC serves the educational community by disseminating educational research results and other resource information that can be used in developing more effective educational programs.

The ERIC Clearinghouse on Educational Management, one of several clearinghouses in the system, was established at the University of Oregon in 1966. The Clearinghouse and its companion units process research reports and journal articles for announcement in ERIC's index and abstract bulletins.

Research reports are announced in *Resources in Education (RIE)*, available in many libraries and by subscription for $42.70 a year from the United States Government Printing Office, Washington, D.C. 20402. Most of the documents listed in *RIE* can be purchased through the ERIC Document Reproduction Service, operated by Computer Microfilm International Corporation.

Journal articles are announced in *Current Index to Journals in Education*. *CIJE* is also available in many libraries and can be ordered for $90 a year from Oryx Press, 2214 North Central at Encanto, Phoenix, Arizona 85004. Semiannual cumulations can be ordered separately.

Besides processing documents and journal articles, the Clearinghouse has another major function—information analysis and synthesis. The Clearinghouse prepares bibliographies, literature reviews, state-of-the-knowledge papers, and other interpretive research studies on topics in its educational area.

Contents

List of Tables and Figures	viii
Foreword	xi
Preface	xiii
Author's Preface	xv
Introduction	1
The Causes and Nature of Collective Bargaining in Education	5
Occupational Needs	8
Among Teachers	8
Among Administrators	15
Employment Concentration	18
Size and Expansion	19
Structural Differences	20
Influence of Educator Organizations	21
Historical Studies	22
Statistical Research	25
Legal Support for Educator Bargaining	29
Summary	38

Strikes in Public Education 40
    The Strike/No-Strike Controversy in Public
    Employment Research 44
        Making a Moral Case 45
        Making a Political Argument 48
        Making an Economic Case 52
        Making a Labor Relations Case 54
    Strike Prevention, Not Strike Prohibition 56
        Soft Devices 57
        Hard Devices 58
        Summary 69
    The Causes of Teacher Strikes 70
        Irrationality and Strikes 70
        Strikes as Rational Acts 71
        Issues Prompting Strikes 76
        Synthesis of Studies on Strike Causes 79
        Summary 82
Costs of Collective Bargaining in Education 83
    Bargaining and Absolute Increases in Teacher Salaries 84
    Spillover Benefits 93
    Nonsalary Benefits for Teachers 97
    Special Constituencies 99
    Rate of Salary Increases 101
    Structural Effects 102
    Who Pays? 104
    Conclusion 106

Opportunity for Research 107

References 109

Tables and Figures

List of Tables

Table 1. White-Collar Public Employees' Reasons for Joining a Union — 11

Table 2. Membership in Major Bargaining Organizations in Education, 1962-1974 (in Thousands) — 24

Table 3. The Effect of Organizational and Legal Factors on the Attainment of Collective Bargaining Provisions, 1970 — 27

Table 4. Aggregate Scores of Teacher Bargaining Provisions Ranked by State — 1971 — 32

Table 5. States with Voluntary or Enabled Bargaining for School Supervisors, 1975 and 1979 — 35

Table 6. Work Stoppages in Government by Type of Union Involved, 1958-1968 — 42

Table 7. Comparison of Education and Other Local Government Strikes by Public Policy and Issue, 1965-1968 — 43

Table 8.	Total School District Work Stoppages for 5-Year Period, 1970-1974, by Issue and Ranking	78
Table 9.	Percentage Differences in Salary Levels, Negotiating vs. Nonnegotiating Districts, 1969-1970 and 1958-1959	88
Table 10.	Percentage Increases in Teacher Salaries in a Subsample of School Districts in New York State	96
Table 11.	Difference in Salary Levels between New York State School Districts with and without Collective Bargaining Contracts, 1968-1969	96
Table 12.	Comparison of Male and Female Elementary and Secondary Teacher Salaries by Level of Union Activity	100
Table 13.	Changes in Salary Levels, 1967-68: Differences between New York School Districts with and without Collective Bargaining Contracts	102

Lists of Figures

Figure 1.	Relationship between State Characteristics, Laws, and Public Sector Activity	37
Figure 2.	Ownership and Essentiality of Corporate and Social Services Proposed by the Taylor Commission	50
Figure 3.	Characteristics of Workers, Organization, and Issues Leading to Strikes	79

Foreword

As the extent and intensity of collective bargaining in education has grown over the past ten to fifteen years, so has the related literature. So today, the serious student of this subject has a substantial problem of selection and evaluation. This work by Bruce S. Cooper is a most valuable aid in this task. He has ranged widely over the writing in education and labor-management relations generally. At the same time, Cooper has maintained a clear focus on three of the central questions of the field: What are the causes of bargaining and union activity in schools? What are the nature and causes of strikes? and, How has collective bargaining affected the costs and provision of education? The result is a review of research and policy-related literature that maintains a cogent and meaningful concentration on important matters.

Perhaps the most important strength of the work is its scope. The relevant literature is scattered and not always directly or obviously tied to schooling. Even though the ties may not be obvious, much of the literature about labor-management relations in the public and private sectors does inform our understanding of the school scene. By keeping a catholic approach, Cooper provides a firm foundation for scholars and practitioners in education to expand their understanding of this complex subject. By the same token, readers from outside education can profit also, especially by discovering the importance of collective bargaining in education to the whole of the public sector.

The comparative approach found here also aids in clarifying the important differences between labor-management relations in schools and in other settings. The clientele, staffing, governance structures, and political traditions of schools are unique. These conditions color the conduct of bargaining and are given their just due here.

By bringing his own well-developed point of view to the task, the author achieves a novel synthesis, especially in his treatment of the causes of union activity among teachers and in his discussion of strikes. The critical methodological comments on legal structure studies are particularly useful, as are those on salary impact research. The discussion of the arguments for and against the right to strike is a handy summary and synthesis of the prevailing points of view on this theme. The summary is clear and well reasoned.

Writing about collective bargaining can slip easily into partisan or ideological traps. This work does not. Cooper maintains a scholarly point of view, avoids simple answers, and presents a balanced selection of the many strong opinions to be found on this volatile subject. By being ambitious and controlled, this review helps move the study of collective bargaining in schools forward and simultaneously closer to our colleagues in the rest of the labor field. That is a valuable contribution.

Anthony M. Cresswell
Associate Professor
of Educational Administration
School of Education
State University of New York
at Albany

Preface

The ERIC Clearinghouse on Educational Management is pleased to publish this bibliographic essay on the nature, causes, and costs of collective bargaining in public education. We have appropriately assigned this monograph to the Clearinghouse's state-of-the-knowledge series, which is intended to provide thorough summaries and syntheses of knowledge in critical topics related to educational management. A previous state-of-the-knowledge monograph on this particular topic is *Status and Scope of Collective Bargaining in Public Education*, by M. Chester Nolte, published by the Clearinghouse in 1970.

The author of this monograph, Bruce S. Cooper, is associate professor of education at Fordham University. He has previously published numerous articles on collective bargaining by school administrators.

Philip K. Piele
Professor and Director
ERIC Clearinghouse on
Educational Management

Author's Preface

This essay began as a short review of the literature on labor relations in education; it has grown into a more extensive monograph. Throughout the writing, I hoped to achieve a single focus, a central question around which to organize the prodigious and mounting research on the topic; but no single theme emerged. Rather, I came to see that collective bargaining, or unionism, or labor relations is not a unitary research topic. It is, instead, a complex field of inquiry, involving, for example, questions of bargaining, impasse, impasse resolution, striking, due process of law, legislation, power, and financial costs, not to mention the interactions between and among these topics.

I settled for three subquestions: What does the research indicate about (1) the causes of collective bargaining among public educators; (2) the justification, causes, and prevention of school employee strikes; and (3) the impact of unionization on school expenses, salaries, and salary structures?

The first two queries for research use unionism as a dependent, or outcome variable, which is influenced in some way by such independent or predictor variables as changes in the legal-political or occupational environment, size and structure of school systems, and the proneness of some teachers to seek the rights to bargain and to strike. The third question above — cost impact — uses unionism as an independent predictor variable and fiscal data as the outcome. So there is some variety of research structure in this literature review, reflecting the complexity of the topic itself.

Further, the field of labor relations in education is a complex one. It stands as a subfield within the larger area of public-sector collective bargaining, which, in turn, is the newest active field of U.S. labor relations. Research in educational labor relations cannot improve without taking into account issues in all areas of unionization.

I have tried to bridge the double chasm between education and the rest of the public sector and between the public and private sectors. In doing so, I sense that educational labor relations are special, for states give particular attention to school governance personnel and finance, and the public views teachers differently from sanitation or police employees. I also realize that teacher lobbies have become increasingly more influential, locally and in state capitals, leading to further politization of school operations.

There are only three major American automobile-makers and one national union of auto workers. In contrast, there are potentially about 14,000 local public school teacher unions and an equal number of possible school administrator and supervisory bargaining units in the fifty states and the District of Columbia, each of which has numerous laws, court precedents, public employment relations boards' decisions, and labor relations traditions. The federal government has so far steered clear of school labor relations, leaving regulation of public-sector labor relations to state and local governments. Thus we are dealing with a landscape of immense complexity. Except for an occasional federal court decision, we have little sense, nationally of where school labor relations are headed.

Much of the research analyzed here is not empirical; rather, the published materials tend to be "thought" or "position" pieces. But such items, when juxtaposed with different or even opposing articles, present the nature and parameters of thinking in the field. They cannot be ignored, nor should they be treated as social scientific findings. They are, instead, the artifacts of a relatively new field of intellectual inquiry.

Despite the somewhat polemical nature of some research, we do know that collective bargaining, strikes, and costs of bargaining are considered by school managers to be their number one headache. In 1976, at the National School Boards Association convention, some fourteen hundred board members reflected this common concern:

> Collective bargaining with teachers emerges as the most-often cited management concern in the nation's school districts. Bargaining was cited more often than even declining enrollment, cutting programs or cutting staff to balance budgets, discipline, public apathy, or curriculum reform. . . .

Asked whether they agree or disagree with a variety of statements about bargaining, school board members gave these answers:

> Collective bargaining will force a disproportionate share of school funds into salaries and benefits: 88 *percent agree.*
>
> Collective bargaining will encourage the allocation of funds to those services which most benefit children: 88 *percent DISagree.*
>
> Collective bargaining will increase the local tax burden on citizens: 87 *percent agree.*
>
> Most (83 percent) think that bargaining "will make teacher strikes more frequent" and even more (87 percent) say bargaining will "not prompt" teachers organizations to be more responsive to the public's wishes (National School Boards Association 1977, pp. 6-7, 9).

This same survey also found that collective bargaining had favorable consequences. Sixty-five percent of board members believed that collective bargaining could "cause board members to be better informed about school district operations," and 63 percent felt that bargaining would "force school districts to adopt more effective management and budgeting practices" (NSBA 1977, p. 7). Such statistics are informative but bothersome. For example, the statement that 88 percent of school board respondents believe that "bargaining will force a disproportionate share of school funds into salaries and benefits" is useless data; a disproportionate — whatever that means — amount of school funding has always gone into salaries, for education is very highly labor intensive. (Perhaps the survey should have asked board members to indicate how much of their budgets went to salaries and benefits *prior* to bargaining.) While such findings must be taken with some skepticism, to ignore these concerns is to overlook valuable information about a growing national issue.

While school board members have worried about labor relations in education, the public has become more accepting. Elam's *A Decade of Gallup Polls of Attitudes Toward Education: 1969-1978* notes that in 1969, when citizens were asked, "How do you feel about teachers joining a labor union?" 45 percent responded positively, 40 percent negatively, and 15 percent "no opinion" or "don't know." In 1976, citizens were asked, "Has unionization, in your opinion, hurt, helped, or made no difference in the quality of education in the United States?" Of the respondents, 22 percent answered "helped"; 38 percent, "hurt"; 27 percent, "made no difference"; and 13 percent, "don't know" (Elam 1978, pp. 34, 279). Thus, while board members were strongly concerned (88 percent) that unionization of teachers would damage the operation of schools, only 38 percent of the public polled felt that bargaining had hurt the quality of education, down slightly from 1969 when 40 percent reacted negatively to the unionization of educators.

Finally, history repeats itself. Much of what happened in industrial labor history has recurred, in slightly different form, in education. But, unless researchers record and analyze the history of bargaining legislation, strikes, arbitration, and key court cases, valuable events will be lost. (I recently called the New York City office of the School Council of Supervisors and Administrators, AFL-CIO, to learn about this group's role in the 1968 teachers' strike and discovered that few of the leaders had been in key roles twelve years earlier. Luckily, the strike materials file had not been discarded, though it almost was once.) Except for the plethora of published materials on a few famous strikes, like the Ocean Hill-Brownsville/United Federation of Teachers confrontation in New York City, we know little about the evolving history of educational labor relations in the last twenty years and earlier. How does the history of local school system development, state and federal policies, and the occupational needs of teachers and administrators influence current bargaining practices? How do labor relations developments compare between states?

Some responsibility for the study of unionization in education falls on the two national teacher groups, the American Federation of Teachers and the National Education Association. But they cannot analyze these developments alone. Scholars, supported by foundation and government grants, must record and discuss the trends and issues in educational labor relations — the largest single area within public employee labor relations.

I would like to thank the National Institute of Education (grant NIE-G-78-0061) for providing funds for research and a sabbatical. While grateful for this assistance, I take sole responsibility for the conclusions. I also thank the research staffs of the NEA and AFT, particularly Marilyn Rauth, director of the AFT's Educational Issues Department, who shared ideas and materials. I appreciate the efforts of Anthony Cresswell of SUNY-Albany and Al Gustman of Dartmouth College, who meticulously read a late draft, gave me additional research sources, and helped me to interpret the data and focus my arguments.

Most of all, I would like to thank my research assistant, John C. Bussey of the Dartmouth class of 1979, whose loyalty and expertise in scrutinizing computer searches, tracking down sources, and assembling data evoke my deepest gratitude. Without his efforts, it is doubtful this monograph would have been completed.

Finally I would like to thank Philip Piele, director, and Stuart Smith, editor, of the ERIC Clearinghouse on Educational Management for their willingness to publish this monograph. The skilled editing performed on the manuscript by Mr. Smith and his staff contributed greatly to the monograph's readability and consistency.

Introduction

In a country where people are judged in terms of dollars and cents and where pleasure is equated with consumption, teachers can be expected to join in the gold rush. We will aspire upward in pursuit of the American Dream and will support labor and professional organizations who fight for higher salaries and budget-stretching benefits. . . . The old-fashioned teacher opted for a situation in which his students obeyed him absolutely and he obeyed his superiors as a matter of conscience. In the 1960s, the American scale of values tilted to favor rights over responsibilities, and postures of the past became irrelevant. The contemporary teacher is as much concerned with respect from above as below. He wants equality and, in the American experience, power precedes parity (Steele 1976, p. 2).

Collective bargaining, strikes, and other union activities have become a common economic and political fact of life in the United States and virtually all free industrial societies (see Sturmthal 1966, also Nolte 1970). Even public school teachers, once the docile, obedient, and self-sacrificing servants of local communities, have taken up the cause of collective action, though, admittedly, they have been among the last employees to do so.

As late as the 1950s, a call to arms such as that issued by Helen Steele above could easily have cost this high school teacher her job. Further, Steele's strident attitudes were not widely shared by other teachers who were either afraid to be so outspoken and militant or who truly believed that such cynicism was unbefitting a teacher. Today, such militancy is common in the actions of teachers and the pronouncements of both the National Education Association (NEA) and the American Federation of Teachers (AFT), AFL-CIO, and is often countered by the strong language and actions of organizations representing boards of education and school superintendents.

Membership in the NEA and AFT has soared to about 2.5 million teachers nationally, making American teachers a large and powerful labor bloc. Such newfound strength permits teacher organizations to bargain local contracts and lobby state legislatures, as the recent Rand Corporation study, *Organized Teachers in American Schools,* notes: "Using a dual strategy of collective bargaining and political action, organized teachers have secured contractual gains locally and simultaneously achieved political successes at higher levels of government" (McDonnell and Pascal 1979, p. 83). Thus, whereas only a short time ago teachers worked at the pleasure of boards of education and superintendents (see Tyack 1974, Lortie 1977 and 1969), currently these public employees are among the most active in exerting their collective power (Strom 1979, Engel 1972, Donley 1976).

A shift in labor relations as major as this one stimulates questions and scholarly inquiry. What has happened in the last twenty years or so that has encouraged teachers and other educators to seek bargaining rights? What does the growing body of social science research and books (Cresswell and Murphy 1979; Loewenberg and Moskow 1972; Doherty 1980; Cresswell, Murphy, and Kerchner 1980) show about the causes, dynamics, and impact of public school bargaining? This essay attempts to organize and analyze this burgeoning field of study and indicate weaknesses and gaps in the research. Further, since collective bargaining has occurred in the private sector and noneducation areas of the public sector for a long time, and since researchers in these related fields have made some extensive studies, it is useful to compare research on educational labor relations with analyses of the nonpublic and general public employment sectors.

A comparative approach has distinct advantages. First, it places labor relations in education in an appropriate framework, one that treats the formalized relationship between employers and those who are employed as a common research issue. Second, comparison points up contrast, allowing scholars to identify the unique qualities of educational collective bargaining. Third, and most important, researchers in education have long learned from analyses in other fields. Since industrial labor relations traces its roots back to the Industrial Revolution in Europe, comparisons may help to identify new avenues of research, that is, questions that have been raised in other sectors and overlooked in education.

Among the numerous issues that research on educator unionization raises, three stand out as particularly important:

1. *The Right to Bargain.* Should employees (and particularly teachers) have the right to engage in collective negotiations for salaries, benefits, and other conditions of employment? Why do educators perceive this need? What have been the patterns of related laws, legal decisions, and local activity? Why have school principals and other administrators pursued collective action? And what are the similarities and differences between bargaining in the schools and bargaining in other sectors of the work force?

2. *The Right to Strike.* Bargaining rights inevitably raise the question whether teachers and administrators have the *right* to strike. What have been the causes and outcomes of teacher and administrator strikes? What alternatives to strikes have been suggested and used and to what end?

3. *The Financial Impact of Educator Bargaining.* What fiscal impact has unionization had? How has bargaining affected the level and structure of salaries for school employees as compared with other workers? Given the recent cutbacks in local school expenditures in many school systems, how have salaries and other costs been affected?

In the following pages, I outline these questions in more detail and, at the same time, compare the growing body of research literature to similar theoretical treatments in related fields of labor relations. In essence, then, this is a *critical-comparative* essay designed to introduce newcomers to the field of school labor relations and to offer added perspective to the more seasoned analyst of collective bargaining in public education. The research materials reviewed are drawn from numerous sources, such as the Educational Resources Information Center (ERIC), Psychological Abstracts, Sociological Abstracts, the National Technical Information Service (NTIS), and the Social Science Citation Index as well as reviews of popular reports and accompanying bibliographies.

This essay by no means includes all relevant materials; rather, an effort has been made to include only the most important research. The several hundred articles, books, and related pieces of literature included are purposely given unequal space and weight. Some are dissected with great care; others are mentioned briefly; and still others are lumped together with works of similar importance. Where possible, I explain the rationale for featuring key works — their importance to issues under consideration. Elsewhere, I hope the salience of the materials is self-evident, for to explain the exact relevance of every citation would overburden this monograph. I believe that the uneven levels of literature presentation mirror the state of the research field, as well as my own particular assessment of the centrality of certain contributions.

The Causes and Nature of Collective Bargaining in Education

Reasons given for collective action among public school employees abound. They include essentially polemical statements as to why teachers and administrators should — or should not — collectively negotiate matters of pay and working conditions, simple explanations of what seemed to cause bargaining to begin, and more elaborate theories based on empirical studies. All these explanations, in whatever mode, may be summarized in four ways; that is, bargaining in education and other sectors is the result of one or more of the following conditions:

The Expression of Personal and Occupational Needs. Employees in all sectors have become keenly aware of their relative financial and social position. Educators, as highly trained, white-collar professionals, came to realize in the 1960s that they were terribly underpaid and that their lagging prestige as professionals had suffered even more because of their low wages and limited control over conditions of employment. Though teachers and school administrators were high on the social ladder, they were losing ground to the well-organized blue-collar workers. The urge to unionize, then, was but one expression of their sense of relative personal-occupational deprivation (Rehmus no date; Steele 1976; Bain 1970, pp. 85-86; Moore 1978).

Changes in Employment Structure. Collective bargaining is often seen by researchers as the result of shifts in the concentration and structure of labor. In the words of David Lockwood, "The most important social conditions shaping the psychology of the individual are those arising out of the organization of production, administration, and distribution. In other words, the 'work conditions' " (Lockwood 1958, p. 205). Public school educators, then, were reacting to the centralization and consolidation of American public schools; the regimentation that resulted from local, state, and federal regulation of schools; and the impact of uniformity brought about by the single salary schedule, tenure regulations, and certification and recertification requirements. In effect, centralized employment appears to lead to unified employee responses, unionization being the most frequent.

Changes in the Purpose and Actions of Educator Organizations. Workers have long been affected by the attitudes and activities of their national, state, and local leadership. Since its inception in the early twentieth century, the American Federation of Teachers, an affiliate of the AFL-CIO, has advocated collective action as the best avenue to teacher power and control. Until the 1960s, however, unionization was not a tactic of the larger National Education Association. The NEA preferred a "professional" approach to employee relations, avoiding the strike and supporting other devices such as "black listing" school districts that failed to treat teachers decently (Lieberman and Moskow 1966, pp. 28-47). The dramatic successes of the American Federation of Teachers, starting with the actions of its New York City local, the United Federation of Teachers, in the early 1960s, spurred the conservative NEA to action. It soon learned to compete with the AFT, organizing teacher unions, leading them in contract negotiations, and advocating strikes as a useful device to gain improved pay and better working conditions. Even school principals and other middle-rank supervisors began to seek collective bargaining, often under the leadership of groups like the American Federation of School Administrators (AFSA), an AFL-CIO affiliate. Thus, organizational leadership is seen by many scholars as a critical variable in the unionization of public school employees.

Legal Support for Educator Bargaining. Industrial employee unions faced great difficulty gaining recognition as legitimate representatives of labor until in 1935 the Wagner Act (National Labor Relations Act) was passed, protecting workers' right to unionize. Similarly, legislation in the states (in the absence of a federal public employment relations law) was important in giving collective bargaining rights to public school teachers, administrators, and other public employees (Bain 1970, p. 186; Lieberman and Moskow 1966, pp. 47-55; Moore 1978; and Kochan 1973, pp. 322-37). Without these legal entitlements, local school boards often refused to bargain with educators. Further, school personnel demanded some avenues of appeal for grievances, much like the industrial employees who were granted redress to the National Labor Relations Board (NLRB) for adjudication of grievances and charges of unfair labor practices. In response, many states included public employment relations boards in their public-sector bargaining laws. Both the right to bargain and the means of appeal, then, are important in any explanation of unionization in public education.

In summary, research on the causes of educator bargaining indicates the importance of occupational needs, employment concentration and centralization, efforts by educational groups to organize members for bargaining, and legal enablement.* We will now examine the contributions of research in each of these areas.

---

* Only one study, that by Bain (1970), attempted to investigate the interaction among causes of unionization in public employment. In this study of white-collar unionization in Great Britain, Bain analyzed four variables and their interrelationship. The first is a dependent or outcome variable (density of white-collar unionism) and the remaining three, independent or causal variables:

D = the density of white-collar unionism;
C = the degree of employment concentration;
R = the degree to which employers are prepared to recognize unions representing white-collar employees; and
G = the extent of government action which promotes union recognition (p. 183).

I utilize two of Bain's variables, C and G (employee concentration and government action), and add two of my own. I leave out the first variable,

Occupational Needs

Among Teachers

Many have assumed, quite correctly I believe, that the suffering of the American teacher is the major stimulant to collective action. While fellow employees in both white- and blue-collar jobs were making gains in pay, political power, and national status, teachers and school administrators found themselves bruised and battered by declining public support, relative losses in prestige, and embarrassingly low pay (see Steele 1976, Rehmus no date). By and large, then, the literature indicates that the growth of educator collective bargaining stems from the same needs voiced by other white-collar, public-sector employees, and private-industrial sector unionists.

Seidman and others (1958) summarize the feelings of many workers about union recognition:

> In their expectations of their union, workers are likely to value most highly the feelings of protection and security that they enjoy — the job security, the protection from arbitrary treatment and from the threat of wage reductions or the deterioration of working conditions. Also important is the assurance that inequities will be corrected, that a qualified representative will present their case if they are treated unfairly, that a mechanism exists for the adjustment of grievances. Needless to say, workers also value the wage increases union pressure may achieve, whether to keep abreast of price rises in a period of inflation, match the gains achieved in comparable plants when productivity and profit margins are high, or raise their living standard at any time (p. 260).

Compare this statement about industrial employees with a

---

union density, because it is the outcome or dependent variable and does not explain the reason for collective bargaining; moreover, the R variable (employer preparedness to recognize workers) is, to me, a corollary of G ("government action which promotes union recognition").

The two I added are *occupational need* — the perception of workers that they need collective bargaining — and the *organizing efforts* of organizations like the National Education Association, the American Federation of Teachers, and the American Federation of School Administrators. The literature seemed to emphasize the importance of these two variables, neither of which Bain used.

high school teacher's opinion about the economic aspirations of teachers:

> As college graduates in an affluent society, teachers have developed the costly tastes of the upper middle class. The average public school teacher is no longer a middle-aged spinster who lives with an elderly parent or a cat. . . . Today's teacher is as likely to be a Mr. or Mrs. as a Ms., may own or aspire to own a thirty-thousand dollar home with full closets, and wants to drive a fairly new car. . . . (Steele 1976, pp. 591-92).

Further, both teachers and other employees value a feeling of control over their work environment. While Seidman and others talk about protection, teachers discuss the fear of arbitrary decisions that affect their working lives:

> We have for years said to teachers, "You are a trained and educated person with a job which is of immense importance in our society." Yet in many cases we have given teachers little voice in the way in which they conduct their work. Moreover, in a regrettable number of situations we have made them subject to the arbitrary and capricious decisions of principals and supervisors. I believe that the response of union-like activity on the part of teachers to increase their knowledge of decisions affecting their work and to provide the psychological satisfaction derived from having a part in the decisions that affect their own destiny (Rehmus no date, p. 64).

Survey research on unionization has not treated the question, Should unions exist? Rather, these studies focus on the reasons why certain employees chose to join, or not to join, a particular bargaining unit. If there is no available bargaining unit, then there is little point in querying workers about joining. If there is an existing unit or a choice among units (see Martin 1978), then the question of the rightness of unionization is moot to those respondents.

Hamner and Smith (1978) studied the attitudes of white-collar and clerical employees just "prior to any history of unionization activity" in 250 "naturally occurring settings" (p. 415). They were testing the prediction "that attitudes expressing dissatisfaction with the work environment are good predictors of union activity" (p. 215). So, while employees were not asked to comment on the appropriateness of collective bargaining, they were polled as to their relative levels of satisfaction with company supervision, fellow employees, their future in the corporation, work expectations, physical surroundings, and intradepartmental friction. Since workers in 125 of these job settings did later join unions, Hamner and Smith were able to correlate attitudes toward work with proclivity to vote for union recognition.

They found, as have other researchers (Herman 1973; Smith 1977; Getman, Goldberg, and Herman 1976), that attitudes are good predictors of future action: "that employees who were dissatisfied with working conditions were more likely to vote for union representation" (p. 420). In particular, knowing the attitudes of workers appears to explain about 30 percent of the variance in unionization levels.

One theme is apparent in the research on why employees seek union membership: the nature of employee supervision. Seidman and his colleagues cite "protection from arbitrary treatment" as a major role of unions; Rehmus recalls "the arbitrary and capricious decisions of principals and supervisors"; and Hamner and Smith (p. 419) found in their survey of almost 88,000 sales, clerical, and technical employees that dissatisfaction with "the supervision I receive" correlated with unionization at a .55 level (significant at $p > .001$ level). Other research places the importance of the quality of supervision somewhat lower, though still a salient explanation for why employees seek the right to collective bargaining. Warner, Chisholm, and Munzenrider (1978) studied unionized social service workers and found that 80 percent joined the union "to get wage and benefit increases" (p. 186); other concerns ranked somewhat lower, as shown in table 1. Although wage and benefit increases were the most-often indicated reason for joining a union in this study, 70 percent of those surveyed were concerned about treatment by supervisors.

How important are financial concerns to teachers when they consider collective bargaining? Do educators differ in any significant way from other employees who must decide to seek the right to bargain? The research on this question is mixed. One school of thought argues that teachers are not in the profession for the money and that external rewards are less important than the intrinsic satisfaction of contributing

Table 1

White-Collar Public Employees' Reasons for Joining a Union

	"YES" Answers		
Did you join the union . . .	Percent	N	Total N
1. To get wage and benefit increases?	80%	85	106
2. To protect your job?	75	79	105
3. Because you believe in the purposes of the union?	71	72	102
4. To protect yourself against arbitrary or unfair management treatment?	70	73	104
5. To improve organizational effectiveness?	59	61	104
6. To have a greater say in decision and policy making of the organization?	48	50	105
7. To gain more independence in work?	39	41	105
8. Because management treated you or other employees unfairly?	36	38	105
9. To gain one or more of the following: challenge, meaning, interests, sense of achievement, recognition, chance for advancement?	35	36	103
10. Because others encouraged you to join?	34	35	103
11. To improve services to your clients?	33	35	104

Source: K.S. Warner and others, "Motives for Unionization among State Social Service Employees." *Public Personnel Management*, May-June 1978. p. 188.

to one's community, helping children to learn and grow, and being part of a national effort to improve society.

One survey taken of a group of teachers provided some intriguing results. The teachers were asked to list the changes they would like to see in their jobs. The results showed that, in order of importance, "lower class size," "better curriculum," "better administration," and, finally, "higher salaries" were the priorities, though the social desirability of such ranking cannot be ignored (Herndon 1976).

Lortie interviewed teachers in Dade County, Florida. When he asked the teachers whether classroom or "organizational" concerns ranked higher on the priority list, "ninety-one percent of the respondents chose teaching-related activities" while the remaining "nine percent gave first choice to committee work on school operations, instruction, and public relations." "The press," Lortie continued, "is toward effort where psychic rewards occur — in work directly connected with their students" (Lortie 1977, p. 164).

It is true that Lortie did not specifically question his subjects on issues related to collective bargaining and that his data were gathered during the early history of teacher negotiations (the early 1960s). But, one can hardly argue with his major findings: "It is of great importance to teachers to feel they have 'reached' their students — their core rewards are tied to that perception" (p. 106). Concerns such as bargaining, contracts, and job protection probably emerge as salient only when employment conditions pale next to the daily concerns of teaching children.

Duke, Showers, and Imber (1979) investigated a related issue — the concerns of teachers over involvement in educational decision-making. If teachers behaved like other employees, they would want greater power and control over the schools and would view unionization as a vehicle to that end. But Duke and his colleagues (1979) found that, despite an ideological belief "in the principle of shared decision making" (p. 20), teachers in this sample perceived a high — and often prohibitive — cost of such involvement based on five factors: (1) "increased time demands" leading to "ever-increasing commitments of out-of-class time" (p. 5), (2) "loss of autonomy" whereby shared decision-making leads to cooptation and control, (3) "risk of collegial disfavor" (p. 6) in which cooperating teachers appear to be currying favor from top administrators, (4) "subversion of collective bargaining" in which shared decision-making is perceived as an "end run" (p. 5) around collective bargaining agreements, and (5) "threats to career advancement" wherein an active teacher "might become known as a troublemaker or a malcontent" (p. 9) because of his or her activism.

It is the research of Alutto and Belasco (1974) that best analyzes the difficult problems of relating the complexities of occupational need to organizational contexts in which bargaining may occur. Their exemplary research study compared nurses (in three diverse hospitals) with teachers (in one rural and one small-city school district) over a wide range of organizational, demographic, and attitudinal variables. The authors' purpose was to test relationships between these variables and "attitudinal militancy" in order to learn if militancy varied according to particular occupations (nursing versus teaching), types of employing institutions within occupational groups, personal traits (age, sex, and marital status), and attitudinal traits (such as trust and professional commitment).

Their findings reveal much about the differences and similarities between teachers and nurses, opening the way for more comparative research among professions. First, nurses and teachers define unionization and "militancy" quite differently. Alutto and Belasco explain that "for teachers, it [militancy] may mean reliance on collective bargaining, in the sense of collective negotiations through a professional association and little use for strike; for nurses, however, militancy may currently entail strike action and reliance on unions" (p. 220). Unfortunately, the authors do not clearly define such terms as "professional association" and "union," an imprecision on which I shall have more to say shortly.

Second, certain characteristics, like age, more strongly affect teachers' and nurses' attitudes than do their professions. Alutto and Belasco state:

> Apparently, younger teachers *and* nurses evaluate strikes and unions more favorably than do their older colleagues, whereas the latter hold a more favorable view of collective bargaining activities and traditional professional associations. Furthermore, age accounts for substantially more of the variation of attitudes toward collective bargaining and professional associations than it does toward strikes and unions, indicating that other factors intervene in the relationship between age and attitudes toward the more militant activities of joining and striking (p. 221).

Finally, the authors measure certain key attitudes, such as "job commitment," "job tension," and "job satisfaction," and relate them to militancy. Here the results are somewhat more confusing and unpredictable. For example, they found that the greater the level of job *dis*satisfaction, the less these professionals are attracted to unions and strikes and the more they are favorably inclined toward professional associations and bargaining. Also, the authors explain, "The greater the degree of job related tension experienced by subjects, the more positively they evaluated collective bargaining and unions for professionals. Rather surprisingly, interpersonal trust was positively related to attitudes toward strikes and negatively related to attitudes toward unions" (p. 222).

Hence, while intergroup differences appear somewhat clear, within or cross-group variation is problematic, indicating some weaknesses with the measurement device. Alutto and Belasco's use of dependent variables as measures is a confusing method: Who is to say that believing in "bargaining" is any less militant than favoring "unions"? Would an AFT member really differentiate between bargaining and unionism? What is missing, it seems, is an adequate scale of militancy, one based on something more concrete and precise than the rather confusing terms "collective bargaining for professionals," "strikes by professionals," "unions for professionals," and "professional associations," terms that do not appear to represent a consistent variable. In all, however, the research design and overall findings are a useful beginning in comparing feelings of militancy between different groups of professionals.

What emerges from the research on teachers, as compared to other employee groups, is a complex and ambiguous attitude toward unionization. On the one hand, educators, like other workers, perceive the need for increased pay, better working conditions, and greater job security (Steele 1976, Donley 1976, McDonnell and Pascal 1979, Rhemus no date, and Lieberman and Moscow 1966). On the other hand, teachers derive much psychological value from pedagogical and professional activities, as well as the general esteem of the public from a selfless professional posture (Herndon 1976, Strom 1979, and Lortie 1977). Lortie, for one, has recognized the tension in the life of teachers and has warned of the loss of public support from strong prolabor positions. He wrote:

Earlier, I argued that status is affected by public attributions of motive and function; occupations which are defined as "service" gain from that designation. If teachers' actions are construed as little more than attempts to get greater benefits for less effort, they will lose the advantage of reputation which has made teaching more than simply a job (1977, p. 207).

Carrying the standard of both an adversary (in bargaining) and a professional (in the public eye and the classroom) may not be totally incongruous, but it has led to soul-searching and confused identities among teachers. If they remain unorganized, teachers may find themselves falling further behind as employees; if they unionize, they may feel less confident about their identity. Whatever they do to resolve this dilemma, recent research indicates that the economic deprivation of teachers is a leading cause of collective bargaining.

Among Administrators

The concerns of school administrators and supervisors are somewhat better documented; their efforts to become recognized as bargaining units separate from the teachers has recently been traced (Cooper 1975, Cooper 1979, and Bridges and Cooper 1976, pp. 306-13). Such current research on school supervisory collective bargaining might well benefit from a historical comparison with the efforts of industrial shop foremen to unionize in the 1940s, following the passage of the Wagner Act (the National Labor Relations Act of 1935), a union "movement" that attempted to resolve the job ambiguity of being a shop supervisor. Dubin (1955) described the supervisor as being "Janus-like," with one face toward management, the other toward the workers; Mann and Dent (1954) said that foremen have "a life in two organizations," making them both "master and victim of double talk" (Roethlisberger 1945, p. 283). Other scholars have called these supervisors "marginal" (Wray 1949) and "forgotten" (Walker and others 1956) people, trapped between management and labor. But it was the Taft-Hartley Act of 1947 that ended the efforts of such groups as the 50,000-member Foreman's Association of America (FAA), for the act legally removed the protected rights of foremen to bargain collectively, a development that is well documented and analyzed by Larrowe (1961, see also Daykin 1945-46).

School administrators and supervisors are confronting a similar dilemma: Should they unionize or go with the management team? One high school administrator in Michigan was hardly bashful about expressing his concern about unionization:

> School boards and their mouthpiece superintendents had their chance to win us over and they flubbed it. They've given us volumes of empty talk about our being "managers" but absolutely no authority to manage anything. They've left us alone and unsupported while they've signed away everything to the teachers. And they've done it all directly — hardly consulting us. Now they don't just want us to live with their actions, they actually expect us to *enforce* them. For principals, the handwriting on the wall is in capital letters. It says: FORM YOUR OWN TOUGH UNION, OR DIE ON THE VINE ("The Brewing . . ." 1976, p. 25).

This angry charge emerged from a national survey of principals' attitudes conducted by *The American School Board Journal* (Jan. 1976). The survey drew from a cross-section of U.S. and Canadian elementary, middle, junior high, and high school principals; its results suggest why an increasing number of administrators have joined the over 1,850 local middle-management unions in the United States. Forty-eight percent of the respondents, according to the *Journal*, "said they regularly or occasionally find themselves *seriously* at odds with their superintendent and/or school board" (p. 25). More strikingly, 86 percent of the principals responding were "in favor of state laws that will guarantee their right to bargain directly with school boards and will force school boards to negotiate in good faith with principals" (pp. 25-26).

The roots of the principals' discontent appear to be somewhat similar to those of teachers: job insecurity, low pay, and poor working conditions. School administrators, however, find themselves in a somewhat more vulnerable organizational slot, as Watson explains:

> The popular picture of the urban school principal is that of a man in the middle, caught up in a storm of angry and frequently contradictory demands. Besieged by noisy delegations of students, parents, teachers, or community residents, he finds himself simultaneously

to blame for poor facilities, too much homework, insufficient time for faculty planning, and students' misconduct on the way to school. When he is finally able to close his office door, he is confronted by a desk full of forms to be filled out and telephone calls to be returned to the district superintendent, the curriculum office, and the personnel department (1979, p. 41).

Although these administrators carry the titles, expectations, and responsibilities of leaders, they lack the resources, authority, and access to the top policy-making councils (Seay 1968, Mitchell 1972, and Sally and others 1979). Caught in the middle, they see themselves as neither truly management nor part of the rank-and-file employee groups like teachers.

The rise of administrator unrest is not an entirely new phenomenon, nor have school boards been skirting the issue (Alexander 1971, Schofield 1976, and Dempsey 1973). The literature on this topic, like the writing on teacher bargaining, is based chiefly on personal statements and opinions. It revolves around this central question: Should principals and other middle administrators engage in collective bargaining for determining salaries and working conditions, or should they deem themselves part of the "management team" and settle personnel matters in a more "professional" fashion (see Wagstaff 1973, McGinley and Rafferty 1973, Ohio Association of Elementary School Principals 1971, Sinclair 1977, Lieberman 1977, Heddinger 1978, Cooper and Murrmann 1981)?

The chief argument used against collective bargaining is that it links principals with the "troops" and denies the administrators a sense of professionalism that is considered essential to being managerial (see Salmon 1972, pp. 3-5). How can a principal be a school manager and a unionist at the same time? The alternative — the administrative or management team — appears equally unattractive, for it seems from many accounts to be a manipulative device that does not really give administrators a real say. Even Paul B. Salmon, head of the superintendents' national organization, the American Association of School Administrators (AASA), blamed the superintendent for becoming so distant from his or her administrators that the management team became an unworkable concept.

Collective Bargaining

"What do principals complain about most?" asks one reporter rhetorically. "That they are members of the 'management team' in name only. That too often they are ordered to implement policies for which they have been given little or no authority to enforce" ("It's Late . . ." 1976, p. 32). Explains one administrator:

> The principal is left out in the cold when the board negotiates with teachers, but just wait until these adversaries get into a hassle over salary, and teachers threaten to strike, or actually do strike. Then the board demands: "How come you principals can't control your staffs? . . ." We might have been able to avert the problem if we'd been invited to the bargaining table to express our point of view. Notes a second principal: "Any principal who tells you he has regular input into the decisions the board and/or superintendent are making about his school is a liar or the board president's son-in-law" ("The Brewing . . ." 1976).

So, like teachers, administrators seek the right to bargain to improve their wages, influence, and occupational identity. School principals and other supervisors have good reason to feel the need for some collective affiliation more strongly than teachers do (Cooper 1979), for these educational leaders could once boast of having real power in days when principals exerted control over staff and program (see Hemphill and others 1962, Gross and Herriott 1965, Bridges 1979, and Pierce 1935). Teachers, in contrast, had very little power to begin with.

In summary, the research indicates that occupational frustration has contributed to the rise of collective bargaining, though, as service-oriented professionals, teachers and administrators express some ambivalence about their needs. Additional research is needed on how educators reconcile their labor versus professional needs (if indeed today's schoolteachers and administrators are even aware of the dilemma) and what finally encourages them to join unions.

Employment Concentration

A second force influencing the unionization of teachers and administrators is the structure of the work force, specifically, the increased size and concentration of the public educator labor pool. Bain (1970), in his study of white-collar unionization in Great Britain, explains that "the more concentrated their employment, the more likely employees are to feel the need to join trade unions because of 'bureaucratization,' and the more easily trade unions can meet this need because of the economies of scale of union recruitment and administration" (p. 184). Stated differently, if employees, like teachers, are treated as an occupational category (with universal stipulations for certification, appointment, promotion, and release), then it is likely that such an employee stratum will form a "community of interest" and seek the right to bargain.

It is one thing to note the impact of employment concentration and structure and another to show precisely its relationship to collective bargaining. Research on this relationship has not focused on teachers but on white-collar workers in general in a number of modern, industrialized nations (Bain 1970; see Sturmthal 1966 for articles by Walker, Lakenbacher, Crozier, Hartfiel, Routh, Levine, Nilstein, Kassalow, and Sturmthal). What these studies show is the following: (1) the increased *size* of the white-collar labor force; (2) the recent *expansion* of professional, service, and civil service employee groups; (3) the recent *changes* in the types and structure of white-collar employment; and (4) the *routinization* of these white-collar positions as a result of job restructuring. It seems obvious throughout European, American, and Japanese societies, then, that the increase in sophisticated, bureaucratized employment has led to the standardization of jobs, which, in turn, has led to collective bargaining.

Size and Expansion

From all the evidence available, it is obvious that white-collar employment has increased greatly in this century, and the labor pools of schoolteachers and administrators are no exception. "In the United States," Sturmthal explains, "where this development has advanced far, relative to other industrialized nations, white-collar workers now appear to outnumber blue-collar workers. . . . More than 42 percent of the labor force consists of white-collar" (1966, p. 367).

Even when one considers the recent decline in pupil enrollment, the size of the American teaching force is large and has expanded greatly between 1870 when the nation had some 210,000 teachers in elementary and secondary schools and 1974 when the number of teachers exceeded 2.3 million. The growth rate has been most dramatic since 1950; in fact, between 1950 and the mid-1970s, the number of school teachers jumped from about 850,000 to over 2.3 million. While the number of teachers leapt ten-fold in a century, the number of school districts *diminished* precipitously — from over 100,000 districts in 1900 to 40,520 in 1960 and 16,960 in 1973. Small schools were often closed; and small school districts were consolidated into fewer and larger systems (National Center for Education Statistics 1976, pp. 7, 20, 21, 22).

Structural Differences

The educational demography of this century reveals many more teachers working in ever-fewer school districts, leading inevitably to the bureaucratization of the school environment (Katz 1968, Tyack 1974, Callahan 1962). While the structural shifts (from informal to formal, from personalization to impersonalization) can be shown, the link between hierarchical control and unionization has only been asserted (for example, Bain 1970). The latter seems logical: Employees are treated as an employee group, not as individuals; decisions are made by school boards and superintendents for the entire work stratum; teachers react collectively, asserting their unitary power, fighting bigness with bigness; top school policymakers react by asserting their authority, further hardening the lines between teachers and management; and, in some states and districts, unionization occurs.

The history of a number of local teacher groups shows the process of structural change and the emergence of bargaining (Lieberman and Moskow 1966, Rogers 1968, Shils and Whittier 1968, Ravitch 1974, Ostroff 1974), though no systematic investigation has been made of a sample of school districts. Perhaps the gradual process of bureaucratization, the restructuring of labor relations in school districts, and the individual changes in teacher organization activity cannot easily be compared across systems. It does seem evident, however, that changes in organizational structure affect the interaction between management and employees; hence, the changes in labor concentration and centralization do interact with unionization in a most complex way. Bain explains:

> Bureaucratization and the density of white collar unionism have been claimed to be interdependent; not only does bureaucratization encourage the growth of trade unions but trade unions by demanding the standardization of working conditions are alleged to further bureaucratization. Inasmuch as bureaucratization is associated with employment concentration, this argument implies that employment concentration and the density of union membership are also interdependent (p. 184).

Influence of Educator Organizations

A third variable that may explain the rise of public educator collective bargaining is the influence of national and state teacher and administrator organizations. The two major national teacher organizations are the National Education Association (founded in 1852 as the National Teachers Association and later merged with national administrator groups) and the American Federation of Teachers (founded and affiliated with the American Federation of Labor in 1916). They are often important in pressing local educators to seek bargaining rights, in using the grievance procedures to protect their jobs, and generally in taking a strong position on policy matters affecting their membership (Donley 1976).

And teacher organizations are not alone in their impact. For over seventy-five years, public- and private-sector national, regional, and local unions have worked to "organize" employees and bring them into the union fold (see Billings and Greenya 1974, Edelstein and Warner 1968, Ulman 1968, Van de Vall 1970). Depending on the national office and its leadership, American unions have pursued the worker with varying amounts of energy and success, though the precise role of national unions has never been thoroughly documented.

In education, the research is highly diverse, only allowing us to piece together the impact of organizations like the NEA and the AFT. Studies of the history of the two associations emphasize the importance of organizational ideology in teacher bargaining, the role of competition between the NEA and AFT, and the possibility of a merger of the two organizations. The research on statistics and other current data (such as contracts) further cites the role of national, state, and local associations in pressing for teacher collective bargaining rights.

Historical Studies

Historians have charted three phases in the relationship between the NEA and the AFT. First, between 1916 and 1919, the two associations were on friendly terms, with the NEA handling the "professional side of teachers' activities, namely, how to improve teaching" and the AFT working to improve "the educational status of teachers" (Shils and Whittier 1968, pp. 22-23). It was not that the NEA members were oblivious to their fiscal needs. In 1894, a woman principal and NEA member said, "If I were to ask you what you consider the noblest work in which a man can engage, you would probably reply, that in which he can do the most good for mankind." She continued:

> On vote, I believe the work of the teacher would stand first, and yet, is this a profession which you desire your son to follow? I think not. Why is this? What is lacking? Largely, to my mind, it is a matter of dollars and cents (Donley 1976, p. 12).

In these early years the official posture of the National Education Association was one of debate, not collective action. The major work of the NEA secretary was that of clerk and discussion leader, not forceful advocate for teachers. Donley explained:

> The NEA secretary in 1905, for example, made no efforts to advance the benefits of teachers. He spent most of his time keeping all records of the association, editing, proofreading, and distributing the *Proceedings*, collecting dues, keeping a complete system of books,

and negotiating arrangements with railway associations for rates and ticket conditions to the convention (Donley 1976, p. 19).

During the second phase, as the AFT became a threat to the NEA's membership drive, the two organizations were differentiated in terms of philosophy, tactics, and affiliations. Between 1919 and 1961, the smaller AFT advocated a militant teacher stance, though it had little power to force school boards to accept unions of teachers. The showdown came in New York City when the AFT local, the United Federation of Teachers (UFT), called a one-day strike and won the support of the majority of teachers in a bitter campaign. Donley wrote the following exuberant description of the New York City developments:

> The union victory in New York City was probably the biggest single success in the history of teacher organizing in the United States. A lifesaver for the national union, the victory brought huge increases in AFT membership, which stood at just 60,715 in the entire nation in 1961. . . . It seemed to demonstrate to the nation that teachers were ready to "go union" — and if they did, union thinking went, could other white-collar workers be far behind? (Donley 1976, p. 49; see also Feldman 1969; Goldbloom 1969; Mayer 1969; Ravitch 1974; and Stinnett 1968).

The third and final phase in the relationship between the two organizations was the conversion of the National Education Association to bargaining tactics. The NEA's change had a profound effect on collective bargaining in education, because, though the AFT may have had the militancy, the NEA had the members.

In 1961, following the New York City victory of the UFT, the NEA board established a National Commission on Professional Rights and Responsibilities to study collective actions for teachers. In 1962, a carefully worded resolution passed the NEA's national convention overwhelmingly:

> The National Education Association calls upon boards of education in all school districts to recognize their identity of interest with the teacher profession. The NEA insists on the right of professional associations, through democratically selected representatives using professional channels, to participate with boards of education in the determination of policies of common concern, including salary and other conditions of professional service (National Education Association 1962).

In its guarded way, this statement urged bargaining, but in the language of professionalism, democracy, and good education. After the mid-1960s, the effort of the NEA in many states became indistinguishable from that of the AFT. Burton attributes the shift in the NEA's posture to the "organizing success of the AFT which began to grow rapidly in the 1960s, largely at the expense of the NEA" (1979, p. 30).

Table 2 compares the membership of the NEA and AFT. Although the NEA never diminished in size from one year to the next, Burton asserts that had the AFT not won recognition for 444,000 or so teachers by 1974, the NEA would likely have enlisted some of them. Or, from a different perspective, had the NEA not begun bargaining and competing with the AFT, its losses, or position relative to the AFT, would have been far worse.

The history of the NEA and AFT clearly indicates the important role played by these organizations in the rise of collective bargaining among teachers in the United States. Reacting to many of the occupational needs and frustrations mentioned earlier in this review and growing out of the

Table 2

Membership in Major Bargaining Organizations in Education, 1962-1974 (in Thousands)

Year	American Federation of Teachers	National Education Association	Total Membership in Bargaining Organizations
1962	71	—	71
1964	100	—	100
1966	125	—	125
1968	165	1,062	1,227
1970	205	1,100	1,305
1972	249	1,166	1,252
1974	444	1,470	1,910

Sources: AFT 1962-1976 and NEA 1968-1974 from U.S. Department of Labor, Bureau of Labor Statistics, Directory of National Unions and Employee Associations, 1975 (Bulletin Number 1937, 1977). All data were provided by or confirmed in personal correspondence from Harry P. Cohany, Chief of the B.L.S. Bureau of Industrial Relations.

increased concentration of employees in fewer and fewer districts (both the AFT and NEA were most successful initially in the larger school systems), the AFT was instrumental in forcing the NEA in some thirty-two states into a bargaining posture. Once both organizations realized the potency of bargaining, they organized local teachers, and the process took hold nationally.

Using a complex model of interorganizational growth, Moore (1978) examined the relationship between the two organizations, finding that "again, the evidence shows the NEA to be a strong rival to the AFT. For each 1.0 percentage point increase in NEA membership, the AFT membership declines .24 percentage points" (p. 212). Moore also correlated the growth of these two organizations with other social variables and concluded the following:

> As expected, we found that the rate of change of members has a strong positive effect on NEA membership and that AFT growth has negative influence on NEA membership. Also, NEA membership tends to expand with the size of the teaching force, whereas AFT membership does not. This is not too surprising since the NEA is an "establishment" organization, and the AFT is a challenger (p. 212).

Although Moore's results are interesting, his interpretation may not be precise. Perhaps if he had studied the decline in the number of pupils in cities as opposed to suburbs and rural areas and noted the corresponding decline in city school faculties (where the AFT is strongest), he might have better explained why the NEA grew and the AFT did not. Moore's data were gathered in 1970, so they do not take into account the last decade of decline in the number of teachers and the spread of collective bargaining. Finally, as the NEA and AFT became truly competitive, local teachers in the larger cities were willing to switch back and forth in their affiliation, depending on which organization obtained the best contract and protection. Hence, Moore's data suffer from being unrelated to some of the events in local schools.

Statistical Research

What does the statistical research show about the NEA's and the AFT's relative bargaining power? McDonnell and Pascal

Collective Bargaining

(1979) examined 151 teacher contracts on key topics such as the existence of grievance procedures, class size provisions, job security issues, and student discipline processes. These issues were then related to affiliation (NEA versus AFT); the results are most enlightening. As shown in table 3, the AFT locals were more likely to obtain "the most purely professional item in a contract — a mandated instructional policy committee at each school site." Local NEA affiliates, on the other hand, "were more likely than the AFT to secure well-defined rules of promotion" (McDonnell and Pascal 1979, pp. 22-23). These findings point to a reversal of the conventional wisdom on the two associations, according to which the NEA was believed to be more professional, and the AFT more like a trade union.

In fact, the research shows that, on balance, one can no longer differentiate between the NEA and AFT contracts, indicating that the two organizations, in the third phase of their development, are similar in their militancy and demands. McDonnell and Pascal concluded that the NEA and AFT competed in all the 151 sample school districts and that the organization with the minority of supporters among local teachers strived harder (the "Avis" effect, so called) to win more from local school boards. Hence, *competition* was found to characterize the relationship between AFT and NEA:

> Possibly, about 1970, jurisdictional conflicts in teacher collective bargaining had begun to peak in a number of districts. Faced with the threat of losing its position as the bargaining agent, an organization with low membership may have had to obtain a strong contract to attract additional members. Why the "Avis" phenomenon shows up only for certain provisions, and not for those provisions which one might expect to have the greatest appeal to the rank and file, we cannot explain. . . . If a bargaining agent has a relatively small membership and a serious competitor, it may try harder to obtain a strong and extensive contract and thus appeal to more teachers (McDonnell and Pascal, p. 25).

It is obvious that both the AFT and the NEA have played an important — and competitive — role in organizing and representing American teachers. Although additional research is needed to analyze the dynamics of interactions among national, state, and local associations, we have learned that as additional states allowed bargaining (a factor to be

Table 3

The Effect of Organizational and Legal Factors on the Attainment of Collective Bargaining Provisions, 1970

Provision	Organizational Variables					Legal Variables		
	Years of Bargaining	Represented by AFT	Proportion of Teachers Represented	Teacher Starting Salary	Propensity to Strike	May Bargain This Provision	Strike Penalty	Goodness of Fit[a]
Grievances	0.506			1.620		1.440		25.03
School hours							-1.252	11.23
Pupil exclusion	0.918*	0.870				0.922	-1.066	14.17
Assignment refusal						1.378		11.47
Class size	0.508	1.012*		0.593	0.805			14.91
Promotion rules		-1.067	-2.337*	-0.967	-1.199	0.909		13.68
Instructional committee		1.102	-0.194	-1.387			-2.230	21.17
Transfer criteria	0.742		-2.315*			1.370*		11.62

* Indicates T<2. For all other entries 1<T<2.   [a] Log likelihood ratios.

Source: Lorraine McDonnell and Anthony Pascal, *Organized Teachers in American Schools*. Santa Monica, California: Rand Corporation, 1979, p. 32.

discussed next in this review), the AFT and NEA competed to organize new locals and swell their national ranks.

Future study of the NEA and AFT likely will focus on the possibility of the two organizations merging to form the nation's single largest union (see Lubetsky 1977, pp. 309-16). Will conditions among teachers reach a point where unification and solidarity override the fundamental differences between the two national organizations? Will two major teacher organizations continue to dominate, or will other, less militant groups like the South's National Association of Professional Educators (NAPE) further erode the dominance of any single nationwide unit? On this last point, Burton explains that "the degree to which the NEA had transformed itself may be a factor that limits its growth."

> The "conservative, independent" National Association of Professional Educators is being touted in the South as an alternative to the NEA, and in Georgia, the NEA affiliate lost 8,000 teachers to NAPE in 1976. Thus, while the transformation of the NEA has made it possible to cope with the threat of the AFT, it has occurred too fast for some NEA members. Whether the NEA can continue effectively to fight a two-front war is unclear; the loss of 200,000 members in 1976-1977 probably reflects a failure in this campaign (Burton 1979, pp. 32-33).

Lubetsky (1977) analyzed the attempts to merge the AFT and NEA in 1974, the details of which highlight the differences between the two groups and the future possibility of unifying teachers in the United States. First, during negotiations, AFT leaders insisted that the merged organization become an affiliate of the AFL-CIO, a condition NEA spokespeople resisted. Second, some NEA leaders mistrusted Albert Shanker, whose rise to power, according to Lubetsky, gave "credence to the contention by some NEA leaders that he [was] a political opportunist interested primarily in amassing power" (p. 314). And, third, problems of internal governance created roadblocks to merger, including questions of representational quotas (the AFT feared being swallowed up by the larger NEA) and the franchise (with the AFT supporting public roll calls; the NEA, secret ballots).

In the end, the attempted merger failed (see National Coalition for Teacher Unity 1974, American Federation of

Teachers 1974, Shevis 1974), but the separate and net effect of these two organizations remains central to research on the rise of collective bargaining in education.

Legal Support for Educator Bargaining

Legislation can be considered both a causal factor in creating public-sector unions and the result of rising militancy among teachers and administrators (as well as other public-sector employees such as fire fighters, police, and local and state employees). Much evidence confirms that the legal right to bargain, established by state law for public employees, is an important, though not totally vital, cause of educator unionism (see Moore 1978, pp. 214-15), just as the National Labor Relations Act and its amendments contributed to unionism among private-industrial employees.

Bain, on whose model this discussion is based, indicates some hesitancy in relating government action to unionization in Great Britain. On the one hand, he argues, "the extent of government action which promotes union recognition is not an exogenous variable . . . but is determined by the industrial and political strength of the trade union movement"; on the other, he found that "at least the government policies which have promoted union recognition in Britain were not introduced because of pressure from the trade union movement" but "to deal with social and economic exigencies created by world wars" (Bain 1970, p. 186). It seems obvious to us that government policies, in this case collective bargaining laws and court decisions delimiting bargaining, are central to unionism, giving legitimacy and structure to the activity of bargaining groups and their employers. At the same time, these laws indicate the existence of a well-developed public-sector and education lobby.

For my purpose, I shall draw on survey and case research that relates laws and unionization. Before doing so, it is important to realize that collective bargaining itself is a *governmental process*, a uniform set of rules and practices that structures the behaviors of both employers and employees (Hetenyi 1978). Chamberlain and Kuhn (1965), as well as other theoreticians of labor relations such as Leiserson (1922) and Commons (1957), argue that the workers' contract is a *constitution* "written by the joint conference of union and management representatives which convenes periodically" (Chamberlain and Kuhn 1965, p. 121) to "set up organs of government, define and limit them, provide agencies for making, executing, and interpreting laws for industry, and means for their enforcement" (Leiserson 1922, p. 61). Slichter explains the role of law and labor relations this way:

> Through the institution of the state, men devise schemes of positive law, construct administrative procedures for carrying them out, and complement both statute law and administrative rule with a system of judicial review. Similarly, laboring men, through unions, formulate policies to which they give expression in the form of shop rules and practices which are embodied in agreements with employers or are accorded less formal recognition and assent by management.... When labor and management deal with labor relations analytically and systematically after such a fashion, it is proper to refer to the system as "industrial jurisprudence" (Slichter 1941, p. 1).

And since the process of labor relations is a rule-making, rule-enforcing system, it depends in part on the rules and legislation of the state and/or nation for its legitimacy. For how else can the two parties (employers and employees) be brought into a governmental relationship that cannot be "walked away from" when one of the parties feels like doing so?

The National Labor Relations Act, enacted by Congress in 1935, established "unequivocal guarantees of the right of employees to form into unions and engage in concerted activity, including strike action, without fear of employer reprisal. It also contained unequivocal prohibitions against interfering with union activity or refusing to recognize and bargain with unions" (Chamberlain and Kuhn 1965, p. 44). No such law for public employees has passed Congress, though an increasing number of states have written laws supporting the rights of teachers and, in some cases, administrators to bargain. And not surprisingly, those states with public employment relations acts (PERAs) are witness to ever-increasing collective bargaining activity.

In 1973, Thomas A. Kochan correlated certain characteristics of states with the scope and depth of their PERAs. He explained: "This paper describes an attempt to analyze public sector legislation quantitatively by developing an index of public policy and then relating it to a number of overall environmental characteristics in each of the states" (Kochan 1973, p. 322). This research is done in three steps, each showing something about the extent and causes of collective bargaining in the public sector by state. First, Kochan classifies the fifty states by the extent — "comprehensiveness" — of their public-sector bargaining laws, using a twelve-item index developed by the U.S. Department of Labor (1971). The scale provides numerical values (zero to four) for the provision for (1) administrative body, (2) bargaining rights, (3) unit determination, (4) rules of procedure, (5) recognition procedures, (6) impasse procedures, (7) strike policy, (8) management rights, (9) scope of bargaining, (10) unfair labor practices, (11) grievance procedures, and (12) union security. A total score of forty-eight points was possible. In table 4, the fifty states are listed in order of collective bargaining legal provisions. We learn from this table the wide variation in state-level policies affecting collective bargaining in public schools, from absolutely no provisions in states like Wyoming, West Virginia, Arkansas, and Mississippi to quite elaborate provisions in the Northeast and Great Lakes states.

Kochan's research on a quantitative index of state legislation is a useful effort, though it has several shortcomings. First, it is outdated. Other research (Cooper 1979) has shown the rise of bargaining laws in several states earlier classified by Kochan as having few provisions (California, New Hampshire, Colorado, and Tennessee). Second, the scaling is, in a few cases, confusing. The strike policy provision, for example, gives the following ordinal values: 0 = no provision, 1 = strike prohibited plus penalty, 3 = strike prohibited without penalty, 4 = some strikes allowed. Thus, a state with an antistrike policy would receive a higher rating than one with no

Collective Bargaining

policy at all, making a higher score a rather dubious indicator of permissive union activity.

Table 4
Aggregate Scores of Teacher Bargaining Provisions Ranked by State — 1971

Rank		Score	Rank		Score
1	Pennsylvania	24	26	Oregon	9
2	Hawaii	22	27	California	8
3	Minnesota	21	28	Kentucky	7
4	New Jersey	21	29	New Mexico	6
5	Maine	20	30	Georgia	5
6	Massachusetts	20	31	Illinois	5
7	Wisconsin	20	32	Iowa	5
8	Nevada	18	33	Virginia	4
9	Michigan	17	34	Indiana	3
10	New York	17	35	Utah	3
11	Maryland	16	36	Alabama	2
12	South Dakota	15	37	South Carolina	2
13	Rhode Island	15	38	Tennessee	2
14	Vermont	15	39	Texas	2
15	Montana	14	40	Arkansas	1
16	North Dakota	14	41	Louisiana	1
17	Alaska	13	42	Missouri	1
18	Connecticut	13	43	Ohio	1
19	Delaware	13	44	Arkansas	1
20	Kansas	12	45	Colorado	0
21	Oklahoma	11	46	Mississippi	0
22	Washington	10	47	New Hampshire	0
23	Idaho	10	48	North Carolina	0
24	Florida	9	49	West Virginia	0
25	Nebraska	9	50	Wyoming	0

Data source: Summary of *State Policy Regulations for Public Sector Labor Relations: Statutes, Attorney General's Opinions and Selected Court Cases* (Washington, D.C.: Department of Labor, 1971); adapted for our use from Kochan (1973) by eliminating other public-sector employee groups (police, fire fighters, state, and local employees) and ranked by score, not alphabetically. See table source: Thomas A. Kochan, "Correlates of State Public Employment Bargaining Laws." *Industrial Relations*, 12, 3 (October 1973) p. 330.

Third, Kochan fails to correlate the policy provision values with actual bargaining, strike, impasse, and grievance outcomes. Instead, he uses the index as the dependent variable and relates the scores to characteristics of the states discussed later in his paper. It is unfortunate that we did not learn from the Kochan study what the impact of these provisions was, an omission Kochan acknowledges at the conclusion of his study:

> One interesting question that might be usefully addressed in future research concerns the experiences in public employment in those states where the comprehensiveness of laws deviates from that predicted by the states' environmental characteristics. Do states which have less comprehensive policies than would be predicted . . . experience more conflicts or suppress bargaining among public employees? . . . In addition, a good deal of bargaining goes on in these states even in the absence of comprehensive legislation (1973, p. 331).

We know, now, that a large number of states have bargaining laws; we also know the extent of unionization in education by state. The relationship appears evident: Legislation leads to bargaining in many states, and local agreements, in lieu of state enablement, account for the rest.

Hirsch (1979) has studied the impact of law on collective bargaining and union membership in a new way. Rather than using the state as the unit of observation, he studied the Standard Metropolitan Statistical Area (SMSA) — a smaller, more cohesive unit that closely resembles the unified labor market for workers. Instead of focusing on labor relations legislation, as others have done, he starts with right-to-work (RTW) statutes (laws usually deemed antiunion) to note the impact of law on private-sector unions locally. Although a different dynamic may be at work in the unionization of public employees under state labor codes and policies, the Hirsch study does provide some important information on the impact of law on unionization. He found that unionization was positively related to the earning level of workers in the SMSA but negatively correlated with its percentage of "white collar workers." Most importantly, Hirsch reported the following:

> Finally, the results indicate that while RTW laws have little, if any, effect on the extent of collective bargaining coverage across SMSAs, such laws do appear to decrease the level of union membership (1979, p. 161).

Collective Bargaining

Given the research of scholars like Olson (1971), it would be expected that laws would affect union membership; without compulsion, some members will take a "free ride," receiving the benefits of collective bargaining without paying union dues. Hirsch's data strongly bear out such an expectation: the South Atlantic area, with the largest number of right to work laws, has only 11.9 percent of its workers unionized, while the Middle Atlantic area (28.7 percent) and the East North Central — Great Lakes — region (33.8 percent) are two to three times higher in unionization. Contrary to Hirsch's conclusion, we believe the presence of these laws must influence the level of bargaining (if the J.P. Stevens experience is any indication). Of course, Hirsch and other scholars face the difficulty of unravelling the effect of laws from the general political tenor of a region.

State labor relations laws have had another important effect, one indicating a departure from private-sector labor statutes. In at least twenty-one states, legislation has entitled public middle-rank administrators and supervisors, like principals, to bargain (Cooper 1979). In contrast, the Taft-Hartley act of 1947, amending the National Labor Relations Act of 1935, specifically denies union protection to any employee who supervises another. If and when Congress passes a national labor relations act for public employees (several have been introduced), the question of including or excluding public supervisors will again be raised (see Cooper 1978).

States with permissive legislation on the rights of supervisors to unionize tend to have large numbers of bargaining units of school administrators and supervisors (1,727 in 1979), whereas seven states prohibiting middle-administrator collective negotiations have none. The few states that are silent on the issue (like Ohio, Pennsylvania, and Colorado) have some local, voluntary, extralegal recognition by boards of education in some 111 school districts (Cooper 1979). See table 5 for a list of states that permit bargaining by school supervisors and the number of bargaining groups in each state.

Do states with bargaining laws vary significantly in their characteristics from states without extensive provisions for collective bargaining in the public sector? Kochan (1973) has

Table 5
States with Voluntary Or Enabled Bargaining for School Supervisors, 1975 and 1979

	1975 (Σ = 23) Vol. (N = 8)	1975 (Σ = 23) Enab. (N = 15)	1979 (Σ = 29) Vol. (N = 8)	1979 (Σ = 29) Enab. (N = 21)
1. Alas.	—	6	—	39
2. Calif.	—	0	—	3
3. Colo.	0	—	2	—
4. Conn.	—	132	—	161
5. D.C.	1	—	1	—
6. Fla.	—	4	—	0*
7. Hi.	—	1	—	1
8. Ida.	0	—	1	0
9. Ill.	6	—	11	—
10. Kan.	—	14	—	160
11. Me.	—	14	—	15
12. Md.	—	12	—	24
13. Mass.	—	100	—	240
14. Mich.	—	75	—	150
15. Minn.	—	110	—	122
16. Mo.	5	—	10	—
17. Mont.	—	0	—	1
18. Neb.	—	0	—	1
19. Nev.	—	0	—	1
20. N.H.	—	3	—	6
21. N.J.	—	310	—	420
22. N.Y.	—	215	—	222
23. N.D.	—	0	—	6
24. Oh.	25	—	66	—
25. Okla.	—	0	—	1
26. Penn.	5	—	8	—
27. R.I.	1	—	0*	—
28. Tenn.	—	0	—	68
29. Vt.	—	4	—	6
30. Va.	1	—	0*	—
31. Wash.	—	55	—	80
32. Wis.	1	—	12	—
Total	45	1,055	111#	1,727†

Dashes indicate nonapplicable category.
* Indicates states where supervisors lost recognition as bargaining unit between 1975 and 1979.
#144% increase   †67% increase

Source: Bruce S. Cooper, "Collective Bargaining for School Administrators Four Years Later." *Phi Delta Kappan*, October 1979, p. 131.

related certain key state socioeconomic, political-system, and industrial-relations characteristics to the scale of state policy provisions for labor relations discussed earlier. He found, first, that states with certain socioeconomic conditions were more likely to pass public employment provisions than others:

> The zero-order correlations between economic and social characteristics and the indices of public sector laws suggest that more urbanized, industrialized, affluent, and high income states and those with rising per capita incomes were quicker to enact public sector policies and tend to have more comprehensive policies in this area (p. 331).

For teachers and the draftees of bargaining provisions, "urbanized" has a particular meaning, according to the Kochan research. He found that the presence of one or two large cities was of greater influence in the passage of public employee legislation than the general degree of urbanization statewide.

Second, Kochan found that state political styles are also relevant. He explains that "a strong correlation appears between partisan (interparty) conflict and the comprehensiveness of the law ... it closely reflects the influence of two-party politics that characterizes most of the northern states" (p. 333).

Finally, Kochan observed that states with certain other conditions in their labor relations subenvironment ("high percentage of unionized workers in the private, nonfarm sector," no "right to work laws," "highly paid public employees," and fast-rising "public employees' incomes") have more comprehensive legislation (p. 334).

The difficulty with Kochan's analysis, particularly in the relationships between state labor relations and state laws and their comprehensiveness, is assigning causality. For example, are public employees' high pay and the rise in their income causes of comprehensive legislation or results of such enablements? Without answering this question, the Kochan study merely shows the vital relationship between certain state characteristics (social and economic conditions, political system, and state labor relations) and the level of legislative comprehensiveness in the public sector. We must assume that such conditions influence the rise of bargaining; as already noted, Cooper (1978) found extensive bargaining in states with enabling legislation for supervisors, moderate bargaining in some states with no public-sector labor laws, and no bargaining where laws prohibited it.

In conclusion, since bargaining, by its very nature, requires the agreement of two parties, one that traditionally controlled the work place (employers) and another with little power (employees, that is, teachers and some supervisors), the absence or presence of enabling language in state labor law is critical in explaining the rise in collective bargaining in education. Additional research is required, however, to elaborate on the two-step process outlined and begun by Kochan. First, an update on the relationship between state characteristics and the absence or presence and comprehensiveness of labor legislation and policy in the fifty states is necessary, using similar variables but attempting to resolve the causal flow problem. Second, research on the impact of laws on bargaining, strikes, grievances, costs, and so forth is necessary if we are to ascertain the reasons for bargaining and the impact of laws on labor relations.

Now that many states have had bargaining laws for a number of years (Rhode Island, eighteen years since passage; Wisconsin, twenty-one; and New York, thirteen), we can

Figure 1
Relationship between State Characteristics, Laws, and Public-Sector Activity

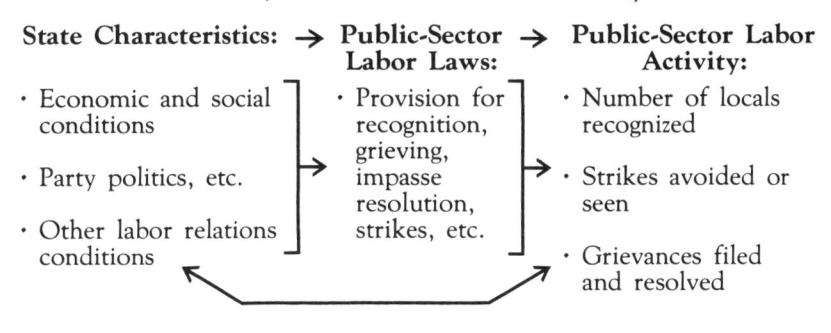

State Characteristics: →	Public-Sector Labor Laws: →	Public-Sector Labor Activity:
· Economic and social conditions	· Provision for recognition, grieving, impasse resolution, strikes, etc.	· Number of locals recognized
· Party politics, etc.		· Strikes avoided or seen
· Other labor relations conditions		· Grievances filed and resolved

reverse the causal flow and ask, What impact has bargaining had on state legislation, as state legislatures have amended their laws to handle more effectively the problems in the public sector? The majority of public-sector employees are now bargaining for higher wages, control over conditions of employment, transfer, retirement, and lay-off procedures. What impact are these labor relations conditions having on the socioeconomic status, politics, and other labor activity in the state? Figure 1 depicts in summary fashion the interrelationships among three major areas — state characteristics, labor laws, and labor activity — on which additional research is needed.

Summary

Our review of the research on causes of unionization among public elementary and secondary educators indicates at least four reasons for the rise of collective bargaining in schools. It is attributable particularly to changes in the psychological state of American teachers and administrators, shifts in job concentration, actions of teacher and administrator groups, and legal support from the state.

First, studies that are primarily personal and anecdotal indicate an increased concern for the occupational life and well-being of teachers, a sense of relative deprivation in comparison to other professional categories, and a desire to increase the power and remuneration of teachers. One teacher stated it succinctly: "This teacher wants to make a reasonable living, to be recognized as a person who performs an essential service, to be considered an expert in my small area of experience, to be occasionally praised when I do well, and to be helped to improve when I don't. In short, I want someone to know I'm alive" (Steele 1976).

Second, such attitudes and the advent of bargaining were in part stimulated by the second condition reviewed in this essay: the concentration of employees in ever-larger and more anonymous work units as a result of the consolidation and bureaucratization of public schools. Educational institutions, like many other employers of white-collar professionals, saw a massive increase in size (Sturmthal 1966) and structure (Shils and Whittier 1968) and the formalization of treatment by state agencies (Hopkins, Rawson, and Smith 1975).

Third, teacher organizations came to favor collective bargaining as the primary means of improving the lot of teachers. Although the small but vocal American Federation of Teachers had long been a militant force, it was not until the National Education Association, faced with a loss of influence and members, began to advocate collective negotiations that the 2.2-million NEA members emerged as a strong force (Strom 1979).

Finally, state laws protected the rights of teachers and some administrators to seek bargaining recognition and regulated the nature of employer-employee relationship in the public sector. Kochan (1973) found that the more industrialized, urbanized, and wealthy states with active two-party (partisan) state politics and active unionization in the private sector were more likely to pass public-sector labor legislation than states without some or all of these characteristics. Cooper's research (1979) indicated, at least for school administrators, the great importance of labor legislation that permits a category of personnel to bargain. McDonnell and Pascal, too, concluded that "particularly significant were state statutes regulating both the scope of bargaining and penalties for strikes. Teacher organizations in states with laws mandating or permitting bargaining on specific provisions were much more likely to obtain these provisions than their counterparts in states without such laws" (1979, p. 150).

In effect, the needs of educators, the structure of their jobs, the actions of their leadership, and the legal environment in which they worked all combined to bring about collective bargaining. The exact effect of any or all of these factors cannot be precisely known, though new research may indicate how these causes affect teachers (particularly in states providing bargaining for public employees).

Strikes in Public Education

Teacher strikes are relatively numerous, accounting for the largest percentage of work stoppages in public employment (U.S. Bureau of the Census 1975, Burton and Krider 1970, National Education Association 1979). However commonplace, such strikes — whether they involve teachers, police or fire personnel, sanitation workers, or state employees — have been the subject of fierce debate and strong action for almost a century, though most poignantly after Calvin Coolidge, then governor of Massachusetts, participated in quashing the Boston police strike in 1919 (see Spero 1948).

Researchers in education have studied the strikes of teachers, beginning with the first major walkout in New York City in 1961 and the famous teacher-black community confrontation in Ocean Hill-Brownsville in 1968 that led to several citywide walkouts (see Ravitch 1974; Cassell and Baron 1974; Wasserman 1970; and Fantini, Gittell, and Magat 1970). As analysts studied the case histories of particular strikes, looking at the causes of these first major walkouts, they became more interested in the details (black communities versus white teachers, blacks versus Jews in New York City) than in the significance of such changes in labor relations. Hence, issues of desegregation, black power, and community control often tended to overshadow the unionization issues. Charles Isaacs, a New York City teacher, wrote in 1968:

> The issue of black anti-Semitism is a major element in the black-Jewish confrontation which threatens to devastate New York City. Yet, here in Ocean Hill-Brownsville, the eye of the storm, the problem seems not to exist. I read in the UFT [United Federation of Teachers, AFL-CIO] literature and in the Jewish press about "black racism," but I have never experienced it in Ocean Hill, and to my knowledge, neither has anyone else on the faculty. But one fact of life does stand out: this issue of anti-Semitism, true or false, preys on the fears of one ethnic group that, united behind it, could destroy us. . . . (p. 11).

Miriam Wasserman (1970) described the same situation — New York City in 1967 and 1968 — not in terms of collective bargaining and teachers' strikes, but rather as these union activities related to the issue of community control. Hence, the needs of teachers as employees were lost to the more poignant cause of black peoples' rights, and the union was perceived as conservative, if not reactionary. Wasserman explained this condition as follows:

> The UFT (United Federation of Teachers) was believed to be an enemy of community control, and the UFT leaders in the schools (chapter chairmen especially) to be fifth columnists. The disruptive child strike in 1964, the UFT-CSA (Council of Supervisory Associations) suit against the specially appointed principals, and Shanker's constant public philosophizing about "vigilantism" and "extremist takeovers," all contributed to a natural distrust of the union (1970 p. 349).

The New York City strikes were among the most publicized because they were among the very first major walkouts by teachers; but they also involved a general contest for power among teachers, administrators, minority groups, and the central administration (Rogers 1968).

Strike statistics are highly revealing, indicating that despite resistance from society, teachers and other public employees are striking in large numbers. In the decade 1958 to 1968, a period when most states had yet to pass public-sector bargaining laws, strikes among government employees increased dramatically, as shown in table 6. Of the 825 strikes during the decade, only eight involved federal governmental employees, with the remaining stoppages occurring among state, municipal, county, and public school employees (White 1969).

Other research reports indicate similar increases: During

Table 6
Work Stoppages in Government by Type of Union Involved, 1958-1968

Year	Public unions Stoppages	Public unions Workers Involved	Public unions Man-days idle	Mixed unions Stoppages	Mixed unions Workers involved	Mixed unions Man-days idle	Other* Stoppages	Other* Workers involved	Other* Man-days idle	No union involved Stoppages	No union involved Workers involved	No union involved Man-days idle
1958	5	980	4,170	7	670	3,160	......	......	......	3	70	130
1959	12	1,570	8,040	10	470	2,950	......	......	......	4	210	470
1960	11	7,070	10,500	19	21,200	47,200	......	......	......	6	290	770
1961	7	1,050	3,440	12	5,090	8,880	......	......	......	9	470	3,000
1962	5	24,300	38,600	21	6,820	40,260	......	......	......	2	30	150
1963	10	4,000	11,800	10	600	3,260	......	......	......	9	250	420
1964	16	16,500	36,800	17	5,440	27,100	......	......	......	8	800	6,800
1965	16	9,890	131,000	18	1,340	13,800	......	......	......	8	640	1,040
1966	78	54,300	128,700	38	49,000	322,000	3	840	940	23	940	3,740
1967	116	118,000	1,182,000	37	10,400	57,200	......	......	......	28	2,930	6,970
1968	177	177,600	2,398,000	46	21,900	120,200	1	123	246	30	21,150	26,600

* Stoppages involving more than 1 union, with 1 predominantly in the public sector and the other with members in the public and private sectors.
Source: Sheila C. White, "Work Stoppages of Government Employees," *Monthly Labor Review*" (December 1969), p. 66.

the period 1965 to 1968, some 578 strikes by government employees occurred, of which 249 involved educators (Burton and Krider 1970, p. 286). Table 7 compares the number of strikes by educators with those by employees of other local governments between 1965 and 1968. In 1976, the last year

Table 7

Comparison of Education and Other Local Government Strikes by Public Policy and Issue, 1965-68*

	Noneducation Strikes		Education Strikes	
	Number	Duration in Days	Number	Duration in Days
Mandatory Law				
Strikes to establish bargaining relationship†	1	10.0	5	3.4
Other strikes	56	6.7	104	8.7
Permissive Law				
Strikes to establish bargaining relationship	20	19.6	2	7.0
Other strikes	34	10.4	16	6.5
No Law				
Strikes to establish bargaining relationship	68	21.6	29	5.9
Other strikes	150	5.8	93	6.2

* Based on data collected by the Bureau of Labor Statistics on strikes during 1965-68 involving employees of local governments.
† Includes strikes where union was demanding recognition as well as strikes where union was demanding bona fide collective bargaining.

Source: John F. Burton & Charles Krider, "The Role and Consequence of Striking Public Employees," *The Yale Law Journal*, 79:3, January 1970, p. 441.

when extensive strike data were analyzed, public employees struck 377 times; these stoppages involved 167,136 employees all told, totalling 3,320 strike days nationally. In terms of idle work days (total workers multiplied by total days out), 1,653,791 work days were lost (U.S. Bureau of the

Census 1976). Of these 377 strikes in 1976, the largest single category of striking employees was teachers, accounting for 146 stoppages and almost 600,000 days out. And hardly a month between September and June goes by when teachers somewhere are not on strike, a condition that has caused concern for employees, employers, and the general public.

Research on teacher strikes centers around three questions: First, what are the arguments for and against the teacher strike? While such research may at times appear moot and academic (since strikes occur anyway), the arguments do influence policy-makers, court judges who may act on strike-stopping injunctions, and the public.

Second, what is the impact of devices to stop and/or prevent public employee walkouts? Like the private sector, states and localities have used strike prohibitions, fact-finding, binding fact-finding (O'Callaghan 1976), mediation, and various forms of arbitration to prevent strikes. They have also used injunctions and police action to stop public employees from striking. Unions, too, have used devices like the semistrike (Kilberg 1969), work-to-rule (for example, not showing up for extracurricular duties and faculty meetings and not answering queries from administrators), and brief and long-term strikes.

Third, what are the major causes of strikes? If the goal of public-policy research is to improve labor relations in the public sector, one must attempt to understand the causes of teacher strikes.

The Strike/No-Strike Controversy in Public Employment Research

Should strikes among public employees be allowed without reservation, only under certain circumstances, or banned altogether? What have researchers on this question written? The arguments revolve around four issues: (1) the morality or immorality of public-sector work-stoppages, (2) the political implications of such strikes, (3) the economic impact of public-sector walkouts, and (4) the strike's relevance to the whole process of collective negotiations.

Making a Moral Case

Some scholars argue that the right to strike is God-given, that if a worker is stripped of the right to deny his or her labors, then the employee is vulnerable to exploitation. Others argue that since the right to strike is specifically forbidden to most public employees, "the willingness of so many otherwise law-abiding citizens to violate and defy the law poses a moral as well as a practical problem of how to deal with such stoppages" (Stieber 1967, p. 67). Thus, writers have mustered moral arguments for and against strikes among public services employees.

Probably the best ethical discussion of strikes is made by Fowler (1973). He dismisses, first off, the absolute right of employees in government to strike (for arguments to the contrary see Siskind 1940). These alleged rights are often based, according to Fowler, on some abstract premise of "natural rights." He warns:

> Highly abstract claims like natural rights always require close scrutiny since they are never demonstrable and often appear to be someone's private value deified into an absolute claim. Moreover, they bear close scrutiny especially when, like the "right" to strike, they turn out to be newly discovered, never part of the traditional notion of natural rights; not unreasonably, the skeptical will ask why such rights were not previously uncovered" (p. 291).

On the other hand, the arguments that public employees have traditionally been denied the right to strike is no moral justification for continuing to do so. According to Fowler, "the real question is always not whether policy or values are traditional or not, but whether they are normatively justifiable" (p. 292).

He argues for the legalization of public employee work stoppages, on the same practical grounds as the case against Prohibition: since one cannot prevent people from striking (or drinking) and since the damage caused by public-sector strikes where they are legal (as in France) has been slight thus far, why not legalize and thus regulate the strike, at least on a trial basis? He summarizes:

Since we have little information, positive or negative, and yet a growing experience of strikes, why should we not move to legalize and thus control them? This seems a sound strategy as long as we remain aware of the substantial normative dangers that may arise from public worker strikes: the possible threat to the sovereignty of the public community, and the possible threat to the "public interest" of the political community, and the possible threat to the values of the merit system. This awareness could be incorporated into the proposed Taft-Hartley Act for public employee unions (p. 296).

Laszlo Hetenyi (1978) argues against the ethics of teacher strikes based on the question, Who suffers? He asserts that

board members and a few administrators might find themselves out of jobs after the next election — a serious enough loss to these individuals, but a drop in the bucket in the total situation. The real losers are the children and their parents. A work-stoppage of significant duration produces severe dislocations in the educational process. . . . The community will suffer considerable discomfort leading to an unwillingness to support public education (p. 92).

How then, Hetenyi wonders, can morality be preserved and the children, parents, and community be served while still maintaining bargaining? Binding arbitration, for one, is not acceptable to him because the arbitrator wants to settle the dispute, "not to optimize consequences for the contending parties or for the public" (p. 93).

Hetenyi suggests three ethical alternatives to impasse resolution and strikes. First, he urges that the public — parents and taxpayers — should be given a seat at the bargaining table as a means to "reduce polarization, and prevent negotiations from ever reaching the impasse stage." He continues:

It would be further specified that when consensus cannot be achieved, the public members of the group, acting as arbitrators, would render binding decisions. It is possible, even likely, that if the representatives of the public were intimately involved throughout bargaining, their decisions would be more in line with the goals of all concerned and less tinged by the single-minded desire to end a stalemate (1978, p. 94).

Other scholars have investigated similar proposals: the presence of interested third parties at the bargaining table (see Cheng, Tamer, and Barron 1979; Cheng 1976a; Cheng 1976b; Sarason and others 1975) and the role of the public in influencing unionized school systems (Kerchner 1980). Yet, to date, most parties to bargaining have resisted the introduction of any additional group at the table, no matter what the ethical implications.

Second, Hetenyi advocates the creation of "councils or commissions (with representatives from all affected parties), which would have the authority to develop and enforce wages and working conditions for a school system" (p. 94). Not only would these councils have final decision-making power at points of impasse, but Hetenyi sees them replacing the boards of education at some point. Other reformers have advocated replacing bargaining with a council: Joseph N. Scanlon suggested joint, cooperative decision-making for employers and employees in the mid-1940s; Louis D. Brandeis designed, in 1910, the Protocols for Peace, a system of boards of grievance and arbitration to settle disputes (see Chamberlain and Kuhn 1965, p. 149). Although these councils are often established with the best of intentions, they have not replaced the rights of employees to speak for themselves in matters of importance.

Third, Hetenyi suggests the most radical way around strike power: the use of voucher schemes to give back to families the authority they have lost to the monopolistic school system. Although his reasoning is not totally clear, Hetenyi seems to be arguing as follows: Schools would continue to bargain, if they see fit. Decisions would "undoubtedly feed back into the system, produce new consequences, which the negotiating parties in the schools would have to include in subsequent deliberations" (p. 95). We assume that he is including the right of parents to change school systems that experience strikes, bargain unsatisfactory stipulations in contracts, or create unlikeable programs. This would obviate the impact of bargaining and strikes in any given school.

Both Hetenyi and Fowler are bothered by the growing power of teachers, particularly when they exercise the strike option. Neither author, relying on moral-ethical reasoning, can come up with practical alternatives to strikes other than Fowler's suggestion of legalizing walkouts under certain stringent circumstances and Hetenyi's notions of replacing the bilateral, closed relationship between employee and employer with (1) third parties that have final power over bargaining, strikes, and, ultimately, the total operation of schools and (2) vouchers to give parents ways out of undesirable schools, thus stimulating teachers and school management to improve schools or go out of business. Perhaps strikes for public servants are not the most desirable option, but banning strikes is hardly ethical and rarely enforceable.

Making a Political Argument

The case for and against striking for public employees has often turned on the politics of these actions. The common theme in the political research on this subject is "balance of power," the need for an equilibrium between the union and, in this case, the city council, county council, state legislature, or school board. Authors making a prostrike case assert that to deny a worker the option to strike is to cripple the employee and leave him or her vulnerable to the power of the school system (Wood 1971). Shanker (1973) puts the argument slightly differently. He says that the political effects of banning strikes in public employment would be far worse than the strikes themselves and explains that "we have paid a price for the process of collective bargaining, because the only alternative is an *unfree society* — and the price we pay for strikes is one that we generally are willing to pay" (p. 48).

The contrary position, one which states that the impact of public-sector work stoppages on the political process is highly detrimental, is often linked to the essentiality of certain public-sector jobs (such as police, fire, and sanitation) and the unfair sway public employees enjoy. Kheel (1969) draws the line on strikes at the point where unions can hold so much political power that society is threatened:

> Collective bargaining cannot exist if employees may not withdraw their services or employers discontinue them. [However, this does not mean] that the right to strike is sacrosanct. On the contrary, it is a right like all others that must be weighed against the large public interest, and it must be subordinate where necessary to the superior right of the public to protection against injury to health and safety (p. 63).

It is the essentiality of certain jobs (and the relative importance of others, like teaching) that gives public employees undue political strength. According to this line of analysis, such employees should not be afforded the right to strike, a case strongly made by Wellington and Winter:

> The trouble is that if unions are able to withhold labor — to strike — as well as to employ the usual methods of political pressure (like political lobbying), they may possess a disproportionate share of effective power in the decision process. Collective bargaining would then be so effective a pressure as to skew the results of the "normal" American political process (1969, p. 34).

Burton and Krider (1970) refer to the results of two different strikes by essential public employees fifty years apart — the police strikes in Boston and Montreal — as a "holocaust":

> Boston (1919). A plate show-window had been shattered. Instantly, the window and its immediate vicinity were filled with struggling men, a mass of action, from which emerged, from time to time, bearers of shirts, neckties, collars, hats. In a few seconds, the window was bare. Some with loot vanished; others lingered.
> Lootless ones were attacking the next window. Nothing happened. That is, the fear of arrest abated after the first shock of the lawless acts. I saw men exchanging shirts each with the others, to get the right sizes . . . good-looking men, mature in years, bearing all the earmarks of a lifetime of sane observance of property rights.
> Montreal (1969). "You've never seen the city like this," said the owner of a big women's clothing store surveying the premises strewn with dummies from which the clothing had been torn. "It's like a war." (*New York Times*, October 9, 1969, p. 3).
> A taxi driver carrying a passenger up Sherbrooke Street . . . blamed the police for "not knowing the effect their absence would have on people." He continued: "I don't mean hoodlums and habitual law-breakers. I mean just plain people committed offenses they would not dream of trying if there was a policeman standing on the corner. I saw cars driven through red lights . . . up the wrong side of the street because they realized no one would catch them" (*New York Times*, October 10, 1969, p. 2, cited in Burton and Krider 1970, pp. 421-22.)

Even public school teachers can be deemed "essential" and thus ineligible to strike, not because their services are a matter of life and limb, like doctors and lawyers, but because depriving children of education creates a kind of crisis, or so the argument goes (Governor's Committee on Public Employee Relations 1966).

Thus, the case against strikes among public-sector employees rests on the public and essential nature of their work; if such jobs were private and nonessential, a walkout would be permissible. The so-called Taylor Commission Report (see Governor's Commission on Public Employee Relations 1966) and the writing of Wellington and Winter (1969) argue that somehow the strike is "alien" to the democratic process, removing from the hands of elected officials control over wages and conditions of employment. The Taylor Commission sums up the argument this way:

> Careful thought about the matter shows conclusively, we believe, that while the right to strike normally performs a useful function in the private enterprise sector (where relative economic power is the final determinant in the making of private agreements), it is not compatible with the orderly functioning of our democratic form of representative government (in which relative political power is the final determinant).

Burton and Krider, among others, have argued against the no-strike model of public-sector labor relations, attacking the two distinctions apparent in the Taylor Commission *Final Report* (Governor's Commission 1966, see also Wellington and Winter 1969). As conceived by the commission, the tidy world of public/private and essential/nonessential categories appears in figure 2:

Figure 2
Ownership and Essentiality of Corporate and Social Services Proposed by the Taylor Commission

Essentiality	Ownership Private	Public
Essential	Coal, steel, railway, and trucking workers	Police, fire, sanitation, and prison officials
Nonessential	Small businesses, certain other company employees	Public education, some state bureaucrats, and local officials

But it becomes apparent, as some writers have pointed out, that there is great inconsistency in the delineations "public" and "private" in the provision of basic services. Burton and Krider (1970, p. 430) explain:

Where sanitation services are provided by a municipality, such as Cleveland, sanitation men are prohibited from striking. Yet, sanitation men in Philadelphia, Portland, and San Francisco are presumably free to strike since they are employed by private contractors rather than by the cities.

There were 25 local government strikes by the Teamsters in 1965-68, most involving truck drivers and presumably all illegal. Yet the Teamsters' strike involving fuel oil truck drivers in New York City last winter was legal even though the interruption of fuel oil service was believed to have caused the death of several people (*New York Times*, December 26, 1968, p. 1, and December 27, 1968, p. 1).

Although the Taft-Hartley Act allows the president to declare an eighty-day moratorium on striking in an essential private industry like coal, rail, and steel, the right of these private-sector workers to strike is not in question. Yet teachers, who are striking against a single school district (with no national repercussions), are banned from work stoppages altogether. The argument in favor of strikes, then, rests on the notion of consistency and the difficulty of interpreting the privateness and publicness of certain jobs, that is, their essentiality and nonessentiality. As Burton and Krider (1970) explain, the right to bargain and strike might be assigned on a more universal basis "because it is administratively unfeasible to distinguish among various government services on the basis of their essentiality" (p. 418).

In sum, the political case for and against strikes of public employees turns on the perceived impact of strikes on the political process. The Taylor Commission and Wellington and Winter believe that harm will result if public workers are granted the right to stop work because of labor relations difficulties. Burton and Krider (1970) write that, in most cases, the "essentiality" and public/private delineations are ineffective standards for allowing some workers to strike. According to Burton and Krider, strikes should be allowed as long as the general welfare is protected through court injunctions against particular strikes. They explain that "strikes should not be banned *ab initio* in any function, but should be dealt with *ex post facto* by injunction if any emergency occurred" (p. 420). Such a case-by-case approach allows the courts to determine the merits of each situation, rather than depend on comprehensive legislative restrictions.

Making an Economic Case

Strikes have been analyzed in economic terms, with a focus on their role in the marketplace. The traditional view is that a market or markets impose restraint on union demands. If the striking union wins higher pay for employees, the cost of products rises, leading to fewer sales and an eventual layoff of workers. "Thus, the union is faced with some sort of rough trade-off between, on the one hand, larger benefits for some employees and unemployment for others, and on the other hand, smaller benefits and more employment," explain Wellington and Winter (1969, p. 1114). Obviously, this model is not perfect, for only 25 percent of the work force is unionized and, hence, unions cannot claim control over the totality of economic life. Moreover, other restraints on unions in the private sector exist, such as layoffs caused by automation and rank-and-file resistance to unionization (see Bernstein 1961).

The public-sector model is believed more problematic, for market restraints are explained as either absent or greatly modified by the monopolistic control exerted by police and fire personnel, teachers, and social workers, and by the lack of production, sales, and profit in public services. Wellington and Winter explain that "government does not generally sell a product the demand for which is closely related to price. There are usually no close substitutes for the products and services provided by government and the demand for them is inelastic" (p. 1116). The nearly total absence of competition prevents a "downward pressure on prices and wages," allowing bargaining and strikes to succeed more easily than in the highly competitive private sector. Wellington and Winter write:

> The problem is that because market restraints are attenuated and because public employee strikes cause inconvenience to voters, such strikes too often succeed. Since interest groups with conflicting claims on municipal government do not, as a general proposition, have anything approaching the effectiveness of this union technique—or at least cannot maintain this relative degree of power over the long run—they are put at a significant competitive disadvantage in the political process (p. 1121).

According to Wildman (1964), Moskow and others (1970), and Shils and Whittier (1968), teachers encounter a number of economic conditions that may encourage them to strike. First, the school district, like other public services, cannot "go out of business" as the result of a prolonged strike or increased costs. State constitutions typically guarantee the existence of public school systems and their accessibility to pupils. Second, since pupils are usually required to attend school a certain number of days per year, striking school teachers may be assured of full employment and back-pay through extensions of the school year, Saturday classes, and/or the shortening of holidays. And third, teacher settlements often include a "no penalty" clause that obviates any loss of pay resulting from the strike.

Other scholars have argued the contrary case that there is a market system of sorts and that striking teachers and other public employees are placed under an economic hardship—both incentives to return to work. First, according to Burton and Krider (1970), "wages lost due to strikes are as important to public employees as they are to employees in the private sector" (p. 433), perhaps more so I contend, since public-sector unions are less likely to have "war chests" to support their membership during a prolonged walkout.

Second, "the public's concern over increasing tax rates may prevent the decision-making process from being dominated by political instead of economic considerations" (p. 433). Proposition 13 in California, the greatest single expression of taxpayer disenchantment with the cost of public services in the nation's history, has undoubtedly had a strong, negative effect on employment, wages, and benefits, though no research has shown the extent of the impact as yet.

Third, in many school districts the property tax is directly geared to the cost of education. Burton and Krider write: "Even if representatives of groups other than employees and the employer do not enter the bargaining process, both union and local government are aware of the economic implications of bargaining which leads to higher prices (taxes) which are clearly visible to the public" (p. 434).

A fourth economic restraint on the public employee lies in the possibility of competition for certain services (Burton and Krider 1970; see also the *Wall Street Journal*, December 19,

1969, p. 1). Education, sanitation, highway repairs, and medical services can be transferred completely to the private sector. In education, in particular, there is the semblance of an economic marketplace, because families can and do enroll their children in private schools (Erickson 1979) or move their place of residence to enable their children to be educated in a different and preferred public school system.

That a loss of student enrollments not due simply to fluctuations in birthrates can be a serious consideration to union leaders is an issue that requires researching. Strikes, or even the threat of strikes, may drive parents to withdraw their children from public school, as has occurred in Cleveland and Chicago because of prolonged financial and labor relations problems there. Such losses in enrollment usually lead to the loss of jobs, the trade-off mentioned earlier by Wellington and Winter (1969).

Thus, in a number of ways, the economics of public employee strikes cannot readily be distinguished from the restraints of the private sector. While few "product-related" market restraints exist, public schools are having to compete more and more. They are having to cut back, face the stark possibility of bankruptcy and state receivership, and impose constraints during the bargaining process.

It seems to this reviewer, based on the limited literature on the subject, that the strike is not a one-sided economic weapon in the hands of teachers and other public servants. Rather, there is a semblance of balance between the power of the teacher organizations to strike and the economic strength of the system that makes a teacher walkout costly.

Making a Labor Relations Case

Is it possible to have legal strictures against strikes of public employees and maintain collective bargaining? Will the parties in negotiations settle at the table if employees have no right to strike? Are there other viable procedures for ending impasse that obviate the need to strike? Research has long tried to answer these questions, often preferring one alternative or another to work stoppage.

The right to strike, in all sectors of employment, appears essential as a means of preserving the bargaining process. Chamberlain and Kuhn (1965), in writing about the private sectors, note that "the possibility or ultimate threat of strikes is a necessary condition for collective bargaining" (p. 394). Commons (1934) concluded: "Bargaining power is the proprietary ability to withhold products or production pending the negotiations for transfer of wealth" (p. 267). Perhaps more important than the "proprietary ability" is the raw power to strike, as Knight (1947) delineated: "Freedom to perform an act is meaningless unless the subject is in possession of the requisite means of action, and . . . the practical question is one of power rather than formal freedom" (p. 4). In sum, Chamberlain and Kuhn assert the following: "Although the strike quite clearly does not inevitably accompany bargaining, its availability as an instrument of pressure is an important condition of collective bargaining as we know it." They continue:

> Management and union negotiators reach agreements when the terms proposed by one party are judged to be more advantageous by the other party than disagreement on those terms. Since a strike hurts management by stopping production and workers by cutting off their wages, neither party is apt to reject terms proposed by the other without serious consideration. Acceding to the proposals or demands of the other party usually involves a cost, but so does a strike, which may be brought on by refusing to accede. The two costs must be balanced (pp. 290-301).

Can such an argument be applied to the public sector and its employees' right to strike? Researchers are divided. Some argue, as does Kilberg (1969), that without the right to strike and in the presence of mediation or arbitration, public employees will be unable to gain the attention of large, slow, and lethargic public bureaucracies. He writes: "As we have seen, employers in the public sector lack the discipline which the profit motive supplies to employers' bargaining process in the private sphere. A procedure which allows collective bargaining participants to forgo good faith bargaining in the expectation that a third party will settle their disputes for them should be avoided" (p. 111).

Other writers feel that there is something special about labor relations in the public domain that somehow separates the collective bargaining process from the right to withhold work. Usually, these researchers argue that the state should mandate some recourse other than the strike as a legal avenue to the resolution of impasse in negotiations. A few have proferred the strike as the ultimate weapon—to be used only after other steps have been taken.

Strike Prevention, Not Strike Prohibition

A survey of the studies of impasse resolution indicates that most scholars prefer strikes to be prevented through some intervention, such as fact-finding, mediation, arbitration, or even injunction (Colton 1975 and 1976), rather than by an outright denial of the right to strike. These devices themselves, according to researchers, become essential to peaceful collective bargaining and the resolution of impasse. No single method emerges from the research as best; nor is any one device universally applicable to all breakdowns in bargaining. As Chamberlain and Kuhn (1965) wrote: "To seek to avoid strikes by using only one technique is to deny industrial relations the full range of possibilities for peaceful resolution of conflict" (p. 411). Chamberlain and Kuhn continue:

> In a democracy that wishes to preserve free collective bargaining, simple prohibition of strikes is hardly feasible or desirable. However, through a number of different procedures, the government and the parties themselves can encourage or induce peaceful settlements. Some methods avoid any explicit sanctions on the parties for failing to reach an agreement. Others are harsher, threatening or applying sanctions if a strike occurs, and some even provide for the terms of a temporary settlement. The first kind of procedure preserves the system of private decision making, and the second seeks to continue union-management relations and to maintain public service with little or no interference (p. 411).

Chamberlain and Kuhn categorize ways to impasse resolution as either "soft" or "hard." Soft approaches run the range from admonition, by which a public leader deplores "the intransigencies of either side or both, expressing public concern over the consequences of particular settlement...." (p. 412), to nonbinding fact-finding and mediation, whereby a neutral and mutually acceptable third party attempts to gather information on the impasse and present "proposed terms of settlement which will secure wide public backing and require the parties to give careful, serious attention to them" (p. 415).

Soft Devices

Research on "soft" approaches clearly demonstrates their usefulness (Doering 1972, Pegnetter 1971, and Yaffe and Goldblatt 1971). For example, in 1969 alone, in New York State, over half of the 800 school districts reached impasse; 200 of them requested and received a fact-finder from the Public Employment Relations Board. In 149 of the 200 cases, "the report [of the fact-finder] was either accepted or was the basis for further negotiations which culminated in settlement" (Doering 1972, p. 2). What were the criteria used by the fact-finders in recommending their resolutions of bargaining impasses? Doering found two: "acceptability" (what the parties will settle for) and "equity" ("the requirements of the fact-finder's notions of fairness and good labor relations," p. 14). Hence, in avoiding the necessity of strike, whether such actions are legal or illegal, the fact-finder acts as both a persuader and symbol of fairness. Doering explains:

> Sometimes the problem of persuasion becomes part of the criterion itself of acceptability. A recalcitrant individual on one of the negotiating teams may have to be taken into consideration in defining the area of settlement, and the criterion of "acceptability" may end up relating as much to personalities and emotions around the bargaining table as to the facts of the case. The situation is peculiar to public sector bargaining. In a private sector strike situation, the personalities and rhetoric of the negotiators soon give way to a test of economic strength. In public employment, impasse procedures are designed to avoid such tests, and it is more difficult to bluff (p. 14).

To be fair, the fact-finder checks the impasse district's past history and compares it to neighboring and similar districts; this process "has the advantage of being both an outside standard and a current one" (p. 15).

McKelvey (1969) studied fact-finding in five states early in the history of public-sector labor legislation and provided some predictions and conclusions about the process. She found that (1) fact-finding "seems to be more effective in smaller communities and rural areas"; (2) when costs are borne by the parties, the parties are more likely to take the finding seriously; (3) administrative skill in undertaking the fact-finding process seems important; and (4) it is unclear whether fact-finding is an adequate substitute for the strike (see also Wollett 1968).

On this final point, the adequacy of fact-finding as a substitute, McKelvey raises the central question regarding this and other "soft" forms of labor impasse resolution: "Since the employer or his alter ego, the legislative body, has the final voice, why should he make *any* concessions to his adversary on the other side of the table" (p. 340)? Wollett has an answer: make fact-finding so painful and exhausting that parties would rather settle than fact-find! He writes:

> If fact-finding is to serve as an adequate substitute for the strike, it must be sufficiently unattractive that employers and employees will usually find it preferable to make their own agreements. Thus, theoretically, both parties should be motivated to reach agreements without outside intervention because of the risks inherent in the fact-finding process (1968, p. 32).

Hard Devices

Other states and localities have attempted "hard" approaches, to use Chamberlain and Kuhn's term, to stop or avert strikes in the public sector. These approaches have included seizures, injunctions to stop strikes in progress, and third-party intervention such as fact-finding, mediation, and arbitration to convince the parties to reach a settlement. Much of the published materials on these devices has been in the form of "war manuals" for principals and superintendents (Irwin 1977, Keough 1974, National Association of Elementary School Principals 1977, Hutchison 1971, Heller 1978, Winston 1975) and boards of education (Sallot 1977, Colton 1977). In addition, there have been some empirical investigations of the impact and effectiveness of various methods of stopping and/or preventing strikes.

Perhaps the most drastic means of stopping a strike is **sei-**

zure, the governmental takeover of vital services and the total displacement of the striking employee group. Such actions are prevented by constitutional provision and have occurred only in dire emergencies such as wartime (Pierson 1955; Bernstein, Enarson, and Fleming 1955).

The **injunction** is less drastic. It uses a court order "restraining specified parties from performing specified acts, e.g., advocating a strike, refusing to report for work, or picketing" (Colton 1975). How effective is the antistrike injunction? What does the research indicate about this strike-stopping device?

Colton (1975, 1976, and 1977) has traced the history of the antistrike injunction and analyzed its use and effectiveness in ending teacher strikes. He noted that injunctions have a long history in American labor relations. They were condemned by then attorney, later United States Supreme Court Justice, Felix Frankfurter as undermining the entire judicial process (see Frankfurter and Greene 1930) and were eventually outlawed in the private sector by the Norris-LaGuardia Act of 1932. In the public sector, however, court injunctions are used often, leading Colton, in his analysis of the St. Louis teachers' strike of 1973, to conclude the following:

> There is abundant evidence that the injunctive relief is becoming increasingly ineffectual as a device for combatting teachers strikes. There has been an erosion of the social and political attitudes which formerly supported the use of injunctions. Moreover, as shown in St. Louis and elsewhere, teacher organization leaders have demonstrated increasing skill in neutralizing the effectiveness of court orders, with the result that the negative consequences of court action often are not balanced by attainment of the intended benefits (1975, p. 4).

Why, according to Colton, was the injunction so ineffective in halting the St. Louis strike? Three explanations are given. First, injunctions lead to "rhetorical one-upsmanship," wherein each side stalwartly supports the rightness of its stand. The teacher association asserts the injustice of having to work under duress; the managers firmly stand on the principle that teachers must abide by the law of the land. In St. Louis, "teachers, at least, found the rhetoric persuasive grounds for continuing their defiance" and staying out (1975, p. 3).

Second, injunctions pose serious dilemmas of enforcement. Strike leaders "went underground," stopping the legal proceedings; others appeared in court, pled guilty, were fined heavily, and became martyrs; and emotions ran so high that "enforcement procedures had to be suspended in order for the negotiations to proceed" (1975, p. 3).

Third, injunctions take time and often galvanize public opinion against management. In the St. Louis case, Colton reports that public opinion turned in favor of the teachers, who wanted to bargain, and against school board members, who wanted the strike ended before resuming negotiations.

> Statements by citizens and public officials began to appear, urging the Board to abandon its dependence upon injunctive procedure and meet directly with the teachers—precisely what the striking teachers were demanding. Pressure on the Board also stemmed from the mere passage of time; as the days passed, the possibilities of completing the school year became constricted, threatening the already precarious school budget. Thus, the Board eventually agreed to negotiate (Colton 1975, p. 3).

Colton also points out that the courts in many states are becoming more leary of issuing antistrike injunctions, particularly when the board of education is unable to show that all other legal remedies have been attempted and that serious harm will be done if the strike continues. In New Hampshire, for example, the court refused to enjoin the teachers from striking because the board of education was unwilling to attempt mediation (see *Timberlane Regional School District v. Timberlane Regional Education Association*, 317 A.2d 555, 1971). And in Rhode Island, the state supreme court found that a closed school "cannot be construed as a catastrophic event" (*School Committee of Westerly v. Westerly Teachers Association*, 299 A.2d 441).

In sum, Colton found that injunctions were not the best multipurpose weapon against strikes, though he did not rule out their value altogether.

Besides the seizure and the injunction, a number of **third-party interventions** are available that are binding, useful in breaking impasse, and thus central to preserving the collective bargaining process. These include binding fact-finding (O'Callaghan 1976) and binding arbitration. As Chamberlain and Kuhn explain, "If the parties are unable to reach an agreement, an outside authority examines the claims and arguments of each side and then fixes the terms of settlement which must be accepted" (1965, p. 418).

Mike O'Callaghan, governor of Nevada, implemented binding fact-finding in his state, a process that required the introduction of fact-finders and ultimately the governor himself to settle walkouts. He wrote:

> The complementary figure of the fact-finder possesses the technical competence to thoroughly analyze the parties' respective positions, including budgetary priorities, to arrive at an equitable solution. Because of the discretion vested in me, . . . I do not have to follow mechanistic formulas in making decisions. . . . In addition, it appears that the procedure as it has been refined in the last five years has resulted in a much higher quality of collective bargaining (1976, p. 270).

The difference between binding fact-finding and binding arbitration appears to rest with the presence of the top political figure, the governor, who is empowered to intervene (as have presidents and the Congress intervened in strikes in the private sector). Governor O'Callaghan only briefly describes in his article the results of binding fact-finding: in 1976, he received forty-two requests for fact-finding, of which only twelve were sent to binding fact-finding, a much lower number than in prior years (forty-one in 1975, thirty-two in 1974, and twenty-one in 1973). He concludes that this diminution is evidence of stabilization (pp. 271-72).

Arbitration in conjunction with no-strike requirements is probably the most common form of third-party intervention (Staudohar 1976), and it is used in a variety of ways: voluntary arbitration, in which the parties to bargaining may mutually agree to use an arbitrator; compulsory arbitration, in which the parties must seek intervention once impasse has been declared; and binding arbitration, which may be invoked either voluntarily or by compulsion. Much discussion has taken place on the advisability of arbitration. Does it hinder or help collective bargaining and impasse resolution (see Rynecki and Gausden 1976; Loewenberg 1970; Doering 1972; Moskow, Loewenberg, and Koziara 1970)? Does it violate the public trust by placing crucial decision-making power in the hands of a private, nonelected individual (Wilson 1977, Rains 1976)? Does it prevent strikes in the long run, and can particular forms of arbitration be improved?

A most interesting improvisation recently has been "last offer" arbitration, in which the arbitrator must choose between the last offers of the two sides and cannot accept in settlement a compromise between the parties' positions (see Stern and others 1975).

The advantages of final-offer arbitration remind us of Wollett's (1968) advice on fact-finding. That is, the parties in bargaining, fearing that the arbitrator will select the other side's last offer, will remain at the bargaining table and compromise before calling the arbitrator. The advantages of last-offer arbitration, according to Rynecki and Gausden (1976), are three-fold: It is "final and binding"; it limits the discretion of the arbitrator and places the pressure on the parties at the table; and it brings the parties together because, in trying to guess what the arbitrator will deem reasonable, often they will settle just at the moment when they think the arbitrator will do the least harm. Rynecki and Gausden explain:

> If the information regarding issues such as comparative salary levels and work practices (which are the predominant standards in final-offer arbitration legislation) is accessible to both parties, they should be narrowing their areas of disagreement so finely that voluntary settlement will be possible (p. 275).

The strongest objection to arbitration of all kinds comes from those who fear the loss of public control over bargaining outcomes. The mayor of San Diego in 1977 expressed his concern as follows:

> If an arbitrator makes the decision as to what shall be paid, then the taxpayers have no recourse to him because he is not elected by them. He doesn't go out and stump. Rather, he will make his decision based on contending offers and most likely hit somewhere in the middle (Wilson 1977, p. 22).

Aside from the political and structural arguments against binding arbitration, what are its constitutionality and policy implications? McAvoy (1972), in the *Columbia Law Review*, analyzes the legality of binding arbitration, which has been attacked along two basic lines of argument. First, the delegation-of-powers approach, says McAvoy, rests on the contention "that the power to make decisions on the appropriation of monies has been conferred by a state constitution on the legislature, which *cannot* delegate the power to an arbitrator" (p. 1205). Courts in several states have recognized that delegating powers to unions at the table is not unlike delegating powers to arbitrators at the time of settlement. The Wyoming Supreme Court wrote, "If the legislature sees fit to provide for genuine collective bargaining, an essential adjunct to the bargaining is a provision for unresolved matters to be submitted to arbitration or determined in some other manner" (*I.A.F.F. v. City of Laramie*, 437 P.2d 295, 1968).

Second, binding arbitration has been challenged on the basis of two provisions of the Fourteenth Amendment. It has been claimed that arbitration panels violate the amendment's "one man, one vote" principle. Also, because binding arbitration forces communities to pay for costs granted by third parties, it denies employers (school systems, for example) due process under law. A court in Pennsylvania has rejected both these contentions. To the first claim, the court replied:

> The mere fact that the arbitration panel . . . could affect the spending of public funds is clearly not sufficient to make that body "legislative" and thus subject to the one man, one vote principle (*Harney v. Russo*, 435 Pa. 183, 192 1969).

Second, although the court did not find that the community was incapable of raising the money to cover the arbitration award, it did issue a warning:

> If we do hear a case in which the tax millage, as a matter of record, cannot permissibly be raised so as to provide sufficient funds to pay the required benefits to the employees, it will still be open to this Court to rule that the Act of June 24, 1968 impliedly authorizes a court-approved millage ceiling increase to pay the arbitration award where necessary or to hold that the municipal budget must be adjusted in other places to provide resources for policemen's or firemen's salaries (*City of Warwick v. Warwick Regular Firefighters*, 106 R.I. 193, 225 A.2d, 1969).

Quite apart from the constitutionality of binding arbitration, McAvoy examines its public policy implications. She asks three questions: Does it weaken democracy? Will it undermine collective bargaining? Will it inhibit strikes? Her answer to the first question is a careful, cautious no; she found binding arbitration impressive in its ability to avoid breakdown in bargaining. Concerning the second, her data on two states seem to show that such arbitration does not destroy the bargaining process:

> Experiences in Michigan and Wyoming indicate that the availability of arbitration does not necessarily deter collective bargaining. In the first fifteen months of operation under Michigan's statute, settlements of 224 police and firefighter disputes were reached without arbitration. During the same period, arbitration was initiated in 105 cases, of which 17 were settled before final determination (p. 1210).

As for her third concern, the inhibition of strikes through binding arbitration, McAvoy found that only one strike occurred in Michigan as the result of an unsatisfactory arbitration award. Hence, arbitration does seem to lessen the likelihood that bargaining impasse will lead to strikes.

Although her data are somewhat old and limited, McAvoy's legal and policy study of binding arbitration is a useful starting place. Her extensive case law citations and careful analyses provide a context for additional studies of binding arbitration in education.

Compulsory, binding arbitration has been a hotly debated issue for years, particularly since 1965, when Wyoming—the first of now twenty states—enacted arbitration statutes for public employees. The empirical research on binding arbitration is somewhat sparser than the controversy over its existence seems to warrant (see Northrup 1966, Phelps 1964, and Stevens 1966). While most public-sector employee unions and governments share a disdain for forced settlements of any kind, fearing loss of control over bargaining and the settlement, the research appears to indicate that "compulsory arbitration seemed to fulfill its main purpose in 1968, i.e., to provide an alternative to strike action as a terminal point in collective bargaining" (Loewenberg 1970, p. 311). Although confined to a single state (Pennsylvania) and at a fairly early period of public-sector labor relations, Loewenberg's study does indicate that three-fifths of the communities negotiated with police personnel in 1968, that almost half of those bargaining "had some experience with arbitration proceedings," and that arbitration was useful in settling even some negotiations where no arbitration awards were made (p. 313).

Chamberlain and Kuhn (1965) comment on compulsory arbitration in the following way: "It undermines voluntary collective bargaining; it allows the parties to avoid the often unpleasant confrontation of their own difficulties, creating a dependency upon public authority. . . . But if the government were to use compulsory arbitration infrequently, as only one of several means of handling large, disruptive strikes, the criticism loses much of its force. In fact, the frequent and regular use of arbitration does not appear to be a very good means of reducing strike losses" (p. 419; see also Ross and Hartman 1960 and Chamberlain 1953).

In a laboratory experiment, Johnson and Pruitt (1972) placed fifty graduate students into twenty-five pairs, simulated a bargaining situation (see Druckman 1967) in which deadlock was assumed if an agreement had not been reached after twenty-five minutes, and fed them information on the type of available third-party intervention—the independent variable in the study. The variation was two-fold: Binding (B) versus Nonbinding (NB); Well informed versus Poorly informed. They hoped to simulate the basic differences between *mediation*, which is characterized by a poorly informed and noncompulsory situation, and *arbitration*, wherein the third party gathers independent data on the case, forms an opinion separate from those of the two bargaining parties, and makes a binding determination.

The results of this experiment were interesting and suggestive of further study. First, Johnson and Pruitt found that "negotiators who anticipated B (Binding) intervention conceded more rapidly than those who anticipated no intervention, especially after the first few time segments" (p. 3).

> One of the ideas broached earlier was that a negotiator may concede rapidly *in an effort to avoid intervention*. Support for this assumption can be found in the high correlation between rate of concession and the perceived importance of reaching agreement before intervention. The more desirable it seemed to avoid intervention, the faster the subsequent concessions (p. 8).

Of the sides who were bargaining, the union seemed more willing to concede in the situation where the third-party intervenor had binding power and little information. Johnson and Pruitt assert that union bargainers were most leary of and

Collective Bargaining

feared the greatest bias under the condition of binding arbitration with less information. The authors explain that in both binding situations (with and without complete information), the union "*often argued* that the third party would be biased against [the union] because it had not moved enough and, therefore, did not appear to be negotiating in good faith" (p. 8).

Johnson and Pruitt found binding arbitration to be superior to mediation, the former involving more power to intervene, more threat to both parties as stimulants to better bargaining, and greater information for making a determination. In summary, they explained:

> The results might be taken to indicate that in certain areas of public interest, for example, matters that involve the police and fire departments or the public school system, labor relations might progress more smoothly, involve less conflict, and culminate in more mutually beneficial results if the issues were made subject to a [binding] arbitration procedure rather than merely to mediation or to the activity of a fact-finding board (p. 10).

This research suffers from the same limitations affecting much laboratory study: its lack of verisimilitude. College students are not labor or management leadership; twenty-five minutes of bargaining hardly replicates months of bargaining; and the perception of unionists that third parties are biased against them is not necessarily accurate since arbitrators are usually chosen mutually by *both* sides. And the bargaining simulation was slanted so that union bargainers would have less movement space (the union was unable to make as many concessions as management). Are such restrictions universal in union bargaining? If not, why have Johnson and Pruitt introduced such a serious restriction into their simulation? Are we learning about union attitudes in general or about a group of graduate students who are structurally constrained by a game?

Feuille (1979) has analyzed the costs and benefits of compulsory arbitration, providing a framework for current conditions and future research on the subject. He considers the question, What are the supposed benefits of arbitration in the public sector generally? First, he says, it is supposed to prevent strikes. What he found is that compulsory arbitration does "substantially reduce the probability of public employee strikes, but the case supporting the need for such a strike prevention device rests on empirically shaky grounds" (p. 68). In essence, he questions the level of danger associated with public-sector strikes—a topic much debated but rarely studied.

Second, arbitration supposedly protects the rights of public employees. This benefit rests on the notion that employers have more power than workers and that "arbitration should increase the employees' negotiating strength until it is approximately equal with management's" (Feuille 1979, p. 68). Arbitration, then, becomes the "visible hand" that offsets the greater bargaining power of employers. But Feuille asserts convincingly that arbitrators tend to reward stronger unions, those that have the least need of additional power in arbitration; the mere existence of arbitration laws indicates that powerful labor interests already have such great influence that statutes to give them greater power are not needed.

Finally, Feuille considers the claim that arbitration regulates interest-group conflict. The common belief is that arbitration somehow ameliorates the tension between management and labor, contributing "to the institutionalized resolution of workplace conflict already begun by collective bargaining" (p. 71). But there is little empirical evidence for this belief, according to Feuille. On the contrary, there is a great divergence of interest between unions, which tend to prefer arbitration, and management, which does not.

Besides these three benefits of arbitration (strike prevention, employee protection, and conflict resolution), Feuille also discusses certain supposed costs. First, arbitration is asserted to inhibit representative government; that is, key public decisions (on matters such as pay and working conditions) are made "in a relatively private manner by a nonelected third party who is not directly accountable for his or her decisions" (Feuille 1979, p. 71). These arbitrators, the argument goes, become part of a burgeoning state bureaucracy, hampering still further the expression of the "voice of the people" through their elected representatives. Feuille counters this "cost" argument by explaining that public lawmakers can shape the arbitrator's purview. Arbitration procedures can thus be controlled in such a way as to preserve both the appearance and reality of the democratic process. Furthermore, since concepts such as "democracy" are not easily defined, it becomes extremely difficult to test the contention that bargained outcomes are more democratic than arbitrated ones, and it would still be difficult even if data on the differences, now lacking, were available.

Second, arbitration is believed to inhibit effective bargaining. According to this argument, arbitration becomes a "too-easily-used escape from the difficult trade-offs that must usually be made in order to negotiate an agreement" (Feuille 1979, p. 73). Arbitration is less painful, time-consuming, and costly than collective bargaining. If the people at the table can rush to arbitration, it may have a "chilling effect," to use Feuille's term, upon negotiations. Thus, reformers have tried hard to make bargaining and arbitration compatible, through devices such as last-best-offer arbitration and screening committees, with little success.

The relationship between bargaining and arbitrating has been well researched, as Feuille reports (p. 74). The results seem to indicate that arbitration does not destroy bargaining. Rather, arbitration settings become the forum for additional bargaining, not its obviation; some bargaining situations seem to require or demand arbitration or something like it to bring about an agreement; and arbitration itself varies with the impasse procedures prescribed by law (p. 74). Hence, in exploring the costs and benefits of arbitration, Feuille concludes that

> much of the debate among students of arbitration seems to result from the different normative premises they hold; and since there is no formula for determining the relative importance of these premises, there is no reason to expect that there will emerge a single arbitration paradigm upon which everybody can, will, or should agree (p. 74).

In reaching this conclusion, he raises many issues for further research: Whether arbitration prevents workers from striking in various public and private sectors, protects employee rights, regulates conflict between workers and managers, stunts the function of electoral government, and, most importantly, undercuts the collective bargaining process.

Summary

The right to strike is among the most emotionalized and important issues in educator collective bargaining today. Analysts have made cases for and against the teacher walkout based on the morality or immorality of the strike, the effect it has on the balance of power between unions and governments and thus the politics of education, the presence or absence of "market restraints" on the teacher strike, and the role it has in making the bargaining process work.

Much recent research has focused on devices to ward off the strike, assessing the relative strength of fact-finding, mediation, and the various kinds of arbitration (see Grodin 1976). Most authors agree that strikes cannot be abolished. In fact, Guinan (1973), the head of the Transport Workers Union of America, AFL-CIO, asserts that "laws outlawing strikes in public employment do more to provoke strikes than to prevent them, and they emasculate the collective bargaining process" (p. 46). Research confirms that the presence of antistrike language in most state bargaining laws for public employees may be dysfunctional.

Additional research on the impact of no-strike versus controlled-strike conditions is necessary. What is the extent of third-party intervention in public school impasse resolution? How effective is one technique—say, compulsory and binding arbitration—over less stringent, less "hard," approaches such as fact-finding, mediation, and voluntary arbitration? Much more needs to be known about the contextual variables (size of district, history of strikes, and legal environment) and their impact on third-party interventions. In turn, we need to explore the impact of interventions on strike or settlement situations. This research becomes increasingly important as the extent of bargaining, impasse, and strikes widens. Furthermore, if additional states should begin bargaining, perhaps under a proposed national public employment relations law, the importance of research on strikes, injunctions, fact-finding, mediation, and arbitration becomes even more essential.

The Causes of Teacher Strikes

Quite apart from the rightness of teacher strikes and efforts to prevent or stop them, one question remains: Why do educators go out on strike? Perhaps the research suggests ways to eliminate some or all of the stimulants to teacher walkouts.

Research indicates that the question of strike causes is dual: What brought the parties to impasse? And what triggered the strike as opposed to other responses to deadlock? There appear to be two schools of thought: one, that employee strikes are basically irrational actions, events that occur when emotions overcome reason; and second, that strikes are logical and rational outcomes of the breakdown in other processes, particularly bargaining and the adjudication of differences. If one subscribes to the first perspective, then one studies the strike as an idiosyncratic act, accentuating the particular event or events that lit the fuse and led to the walkout.

If one believes that strikes are rational, and thus predictable, then one attempts, as some researchers have done, to correlate certain social, structural, and policy variables with the advent of strikes. Finally, the prevention of strikes is possible only if one can grasp their causes. As the research on the question of causes of teacher strikes indicates, there are many reasons, which have been examined in many different ways.

Irrationality and Strikes

As discussed earlier, many of the case studies of teacher strikes, particularly in New York City (see Ravitch 1974, Vagts and Stone 1969), place the cause of strikes on some form of emotional outburst, some form of frustration based on either a group's sense of deprivation (Batchelder 1965, Friedman 1966, Murphy 1971) or individual feelings of loss (Yerkovich 1967, Neal 1971). The common denominator in all these analyses is that teaching is an oppressed occupation and strikes are attempts to improve the sense of efficacy. Bruno and Nelken describe the theory that frustration motivates teacher behavior:

> Advocates of the frustration theories . . . present the teachers' restlessness as due to frustration; frustration with unrealistic salaries, overwhelming class loads, heavy pressures, non-teaching chores, and a general want of conditions for effective education. The basic tenet of the frustration model is that today's teacher is better prepared and has a better education than teachers of previous generations. Therefore, the teacher notices and responds to the above problems in greater depth and becomes more frustrated when they are not successfully resolved (1975, p. 67).

But these general feelings of malaise and frustration hardly explain why one group of teachers walks out and another does not. If anything, teachers of a generation ago were more oppressed than those of today. They were more easily fired (Tyack 1970, p. 14), more poorly paid, and tended to remain teachers for shorter periods of time (Lortie 1977, p. 8). (Perhaps studies of heart attacks, alcoholism, suicides, absenteeism, and resignations among teachers would address questions of personal frustration better than do those on collective strikes.)

Teachers also go on strike because their leadership asks them to; it is an organizational decision rather than a personal one. And since strikes are almost always illegal in public education, the question is transformed: What makes teachers and other public employees vote to break the law? Is it rational or irrational? Like any form of civil disobedience, it possesses elements of both. It is rational in that employees must calculate the costs of loss of income, prestige, and legal righteousness. It is irrational in that some emotionality and risk-taking are required (Isaacs 1968, Spero 1948).

Strikes as Rational Acts

The vast body of research on causes of strikes treats them as predictable and understandable events that can be explained by a causal model. Social scientists have sought to construct such a model by correlating actual strike activity or reported proclivity to strike with certain personal variables (for example, age, sex, race, political leanings, cynicism), structural variables (size of union, level of centralization or decentralization of the union, level of school bureaucracy), and issues at impasse (salaries, fringe benefits, layoff procedures, and grievance language).

The level of rationality and certitude of some of these scholars is highlighted by comments of Bruno and Nelken (1975). Based on their analysis of questionnaires from 688 teachers in a single county (with only a 34 percent return rate), the authors suggested that management might use their results to hire only staff who were not prone to strike:

> The model . . . allows policy decisions to be made in the area of allocation of resources to those determinants which prevent or lessen the probability of strike behavior. In addition, it can provide insight for an administrator in hiring practices which would *lessen the hiring* of those with more propensity to strike. For the "opposition," the model can also be used by the union organizer for determining the most militant teachers and those to whom he ought to direct attention in organizing teachers of a district to strike (p. 69).

The dependent variable in this study was dichotomous: "Yes, I will strike/no, I won't." The predictor variables influencing "teacher activism, militancy, and propensity to strike" (p. 72) included the teachers' salaries, sex, age, membership in teacher organizations, liberal versus conservative views; the school's authority structure; and the district's size. The results of the study were as follows:

1. *Political leaning:* the more politically conservative a teacher is, the less his propensity to strike.
2. *Teacher sex:* a female teacher has less propensity to strike than a male teacher.
3. *Teacher cynicism:* the less cynical teacher has less propensity to strike.
4. *Teacher "moonlighting":* a teacher who does not have an outside job in addition to his teaching has a lesser propensity to strike.
5. *Teacher colleague orientation:* a teacher whose colleagues' orientation toward administration is more positive has a lesser propensity to strike.
6. *Teacher orientation to public:* a teacher with a strong administrator orientation has less propensity to strike.
7. *Teacher age:* an older teacher has less propensity to strike than a younger teacher.
8. *Teaching load:* the teacher with a lighter teaching load has less propensity to strike.
9. *Total teacher family income:* the greater the total family income, the less the teacher's propensity to strike.
10. *Teacher morale:* the higher the teacher's morale, the less the teacher's propensity to strike.
11. *Teacher attitude toward peer evaluation:* the less the teacher's belief in peer evaluation the less his propensity to strike (p. 82).

Of the eleven predictor variables in this study, three stood out: sex, political leaning, and moonlighting. Hence, being male, liberal, and poorly paid yet ambitious (holding a second job) were found by Bruno and Nelken to be the best predictors of strike behavior. The authors admit, however, that the propensity to strike is not the same thing as making that decision: "The study was conducted on a teacher population which had not actually participated in a strike (had a workstoppage). The strike responses of participants were only hypothetical and best judgments," not real experiences (1975, p. 38).

Nasstrom and Brelsford (1976) compared two school districts in Indiana in terms of the militancy of their teachers. The findings appear to contradict those of Bruno and Nelken in one school district but not in the other. "In Valley [school district], there was no evidence of significant differences between men and women in their attitudes toward strikes, but in Midland, a significant difference existed, with females indicating far more opposition to strikes than males" (p. 251). Other independent variables also distinguished the Nasstrom and Brelsford study from that of Bruno and Nelken. Whereas Bruno and Nelken found that younger teachers were more strike prone, Nasstrom and Brelsford learned that in one district, Valley, "no significant difference in attitude toward strikes was evident according to age" (p. 251). And although the former study noted that teachers with lower incomes were more likely to advocate a strike, Nasstrom and Brelsford's report states: "Not even the substantially lower salary increase of teachers in Midland, who depended on the board's judgment, led them into the militancy characteristic of Valley teachers" (p. 253).

It is evident from these and other studies (Belasco, Alutto, and Glassman 1971, Phillips and Conforti 1972) that teacher characteristics and background are inadequate predictors of the propensity to strike. Also, because few, if any, of the teachers in these studies had actually walked off the job, one can conclude that there is a big difference between proclivity and action. Is it not also likely that personal characteristics assume less importance in the face of strong environmental pressures, such as massive layoffs, drastic cuts in salaries, and perceived managerial caprice? Teachers in conservative centers like Savannah and New Orleans have walked out, though their personal characteristics (conservative politics, gender, cynicism scale) might have put them in the no-strike category. In essence, such predictors of strike remain just that, predictors, not certainties about strike behavior.

Finally, the strike is a collective effort, not a personal one. A bargaining unit goes on strike, not any given teacher, though teachers and other employees may vary as to their willingness to walk out and stay out. Perhaps the indicators of strike propensity can better be understood through studies of strike compliance.

Other scholars have related the strike to structural variables within the union. In a study of the private sector, for example, Roomkin (1972) related the "internal structure of national unions to the collective bargaining activities of affiliated subordinate organizations, such as local unions" (p. 198). He observed the correlation of several factors with the incidence of strikes by locals. These factors included national approval of subordinate contracts, national approval of all strikes by subordinates, number of members in union, and the existence of intermediate levels in the union structure (a proxy measure of the "relative degree of centralization within national unions").

Roomkin found the following: (1) Strikes of locals are less likely when national unions require explicit approval; (2) strikes are negatively related to the interval between national conventions; (3) larger national unions tend to have more means of control over locals, minimizing the power of larger locals; and (4) unions with intermediate structures between national and local units have more strikes, perhaps because these bodies "alter the distribution of power within the union, probably making it more difficult for a national to control subordinate bodies" (p. 214).

Roomkin pointed out, however, that most of the relationships were not statistically significant: "The statistically insignificant performance of NAC [national approval of contracts], NAS [national approval of local strikes], and STR [existence of an intermediate structure]... detracts from the overall credibility of our hypotheses about internal control and compels further analysis" (Roomkin 1972, p. 208). Others, too, have attempted to use structural variables to study the strike levels (see Tannenbaum 1965), though with similar mixed results.

James R. Perry (1977) correlated the frequency, participation, and duration of strikes with certain key independent variables: earnings ratio of employees, income change between 1960 and 1970, percentage of unionization, previous strike activities, and state legal policy. He hoped to show that certain state legal policy outcomes influence the frequency of strikes among public employees (teachers, local government employees excluding police or fire, and state government workers). His findings, summarized below, were weak to mixed.

(1) *Earnings ratios* were negatively correlated with strikes, leading him to conclude that well-compensated unions may press for more, whereas lower-wage groups may not (see also Wellington and Winter 1970).

(2) *Income change* was also negatively correlated with strikes, particularly in the case of teachers. To Perry this meant that "strike participation tends to be more widespread in those states where state employee earnings have increased most rapidly but where the relative position of state government employees vis-a-vis other public employees had undergone little change" (p. 277).

(3) *Employee intensity*—number of employees per job site—correlated with only three strike variables, implying a lack of relationship.

(4) *Unionization* strongly correlated with strikes, as might be expected since collective bargaining and strikes are clearly related.

(5) *Previous strike activity* did not correlate significantly with any local employee strike measures (p. 278).

(6) *Legal policies* also had a mixed outcome; no relationship was evident for state government employees, but the policies were found to be "significantly related to strike frequency among both teachers and local employees" (p. 278).

Perry's study found little relationship between certain state policy variables and the frequency of strikes, but he admits that the finding may have resulted in part from methodological problems. He concludes:

> Although the analysis suggests that state laws did not have the hypothesized effect as an intervening variable, they had *some* impact on strike activity, although this varied among groups. These differences may originate in variation among the three groups in the professional composition of their workforces, in the amounts of pressure exerted to prevent strikes and in the orderliness of transition to collective bargaining (p. 281).

Again, we learn that strikes cannot easily be predicted from some megameasure or statewide trends. Perry did not publish enough data for the reader to evaluate why such relationships were not observed. Although state policies may not have influenced strikes, one can think of other measures of state policies, such as binding arbitration, that might determine them.

Issues Prompting Strikes

Finally, researchers have attempted to analyze the causes of strikes by studying the issues reported to have prompted the walkouts, such as disagreements over wages, rights to bargain, and layoff provisions. The research findings in this area are somewhat more consistent and meaningful than those reported earlier. Perhaps the advantage of this approach lies in the direct relationship between some particular event (for example, impasse over a wage package) and a strike. Furthermore, strike issues may change over time, starting with strikes for recognition and the right to bargain, moving to controversies over wages and fringe benefits, and, more recently perhaps, focusing on layoffs, seniority, and general job security. Available research indicates something of a progression, though adequate longitudinal studies of strike-causing issues have yet to be done.

White (1969) investigated the causes of strikes in government between 1958 and 1968, a vital period when collective bargaining for public employees was just beginning. She found that the annual frequency of strikes had increased from 15 to

245 in ten years. Whereas private-sector walkouts in this period increased significantly, their increase in the public sector was far greater. Strikes of public employees constituted only .4 percent of all strikes in 1958, yet ten years later constituted 5.0 percent. Why, according to White's analysis, did government employees strike?

> The issues that prompted government workers to leave their jobs during the past decade (1958-68) were generally similar to strike issues in private industry. In both sectors, higher wages and supplementary benefits are the most frequent cause of striking, while job security is least likely to induce action. Government employees, however, are more likely to strike to secure official recognition of their unions than are their counterparts in private industry. Employees in the private sector, many of whom work for firms that have recognized and bargained with unions for decades, strike over matters of administration as frequently as they do over union organization. . . . During the same period, almost 22 percent of all walkouts in government involved problems of union organization and security, while administration matters accounted for only 13 percent of total.
>
> Wage issues have become even more important in government in recent years. From 1962 to 1965, this issue accounted for 54 percent of government stoppages and somewhat higher proportions of workers and man-days of idleness (White 1969, p. 66).

Besides presenting general data on all federal, state, and local employees, White also singles out teachers and library employees, who made up almost half of all the personnel involved in public-sector walkouts. "Teachers have sought not only higher salaries but also the right to participate in decisions on how, what, and where they were to teach, and in determining the best allocation of usually limited school budgets" (p. 65).

White's conclusions are supported by research conducted almost ten years later. Torrence (1976) explains why teachers struck in the period 1970 to 1975: "Wages, of course" (p. 29). Teachers in the United States engaged in 898 strikes between 1970 and 1974; the issue of wage changes (increases) was the cause in 69 percent of the cases. In total, 411,500 teachers walked off the job, resulting in 4.173 million idle work-days in public schools in five years. Table 8 indicates that "union organization and security ranked a weak second, with 75 strikes resulting from this dispute and about a half-million days lost" (Torrence 1976, p. 29).

Collective Bargaining

Table 8

Total School District Work Stoppages for 5-Year Period, 1970-1974, by Issue and Ranking

	No. of Stoppages	Rank	No. of Workers (in thousands)	Rank	No. of Man-Days Idle (in thousands)	Rank
General Wage Changes	617	1	411.5	1	4,173.5	1
Supplementary Benefits	10	8	1.0	9	3.3	9
Wage Adjustments	21	5	12.2	5	57.5	4
Hours of Work	5	9	2.1	8	7.6	8
Other Contractual Matters	15	7	5.3	7	31.2	7
Union Org. & Security	75	3	32.8	2	513.6	2
Job Security	53	4	18.0	3	132.1	3
Plant Administration	78	2	14.7	4	50.8	5
Other Working Conditions	18	6	7.4	6	34.2	6
Interunion and Intraunion Affairs	1	11	(1)	11	.2	11
Not Reported	5	9	.4	10	.6	10
Total	898		505.4		5,004.6	

Source: U.S. Department of Labor; printed in Torrence 1976, p. 29.

Other authors, too, have attempted to understand impasse and strike in terms of the issues. O'Connell and Heller (1976), for example, in their survey of nineteen randomly selected school districts in New York State, found at least five major issues about which boards of education and teachers strongly disagree, issues that might lead to an impasse and a strike: (1) Shared decision-making on education policy and working conditions, (2) supplemental benefits including time off and fringe benefits, (3) merit pay and accountability, (4) tenure and job security, and (5) increased school duties (p. 21). Noticeably missing from this list is the issue of higher wages, which was not an issue considered by O'Connell and Heller in this study.

Finally, the most recent data on strike causes released by the

National Education Association show that in 1978-79 there were "176 teacher walkouts in 23 states and the District of Columbia, 143 of these by NEA affiliates, 29 by AFT, and 4 AAUP," with wages and class size the key issues. "So economic issues and class load have topped the list of strike issues, followed by such old standbys as discipline, school board refusal to negotiate or efforts to roll back previous gains, job security, contract duration, planning time, and evaluation of teachers" (National Education Association 1979, p. 2). Although no data were provided, these news release items appear consistent with the findings of other research on issues that lead to strikes.

Synthesis of Studies on Strike Causes

Do we now know why teachers strike? Is it possible somehow to integrate the three approaches used in research on this question? An attempt to relate teacher characteristics and union structure to the issues that might lead to impasse and strike is displayed in figure 3.

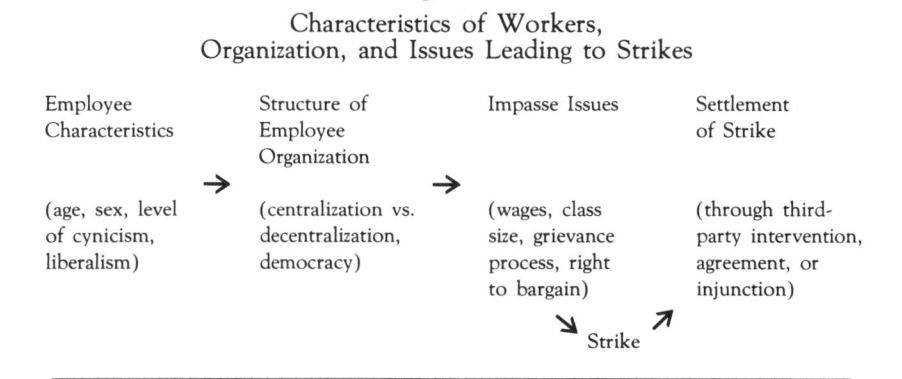

Figure 3
Characteristics of Workers,
Organization, and Issues Leading to Strikes

Employee Characteristics	Structure of Employee Organization	Impasse Issues	Settlement of Strike
(age, sex, level of cynicism, liberalism)	(centralization vs. decentralization, democracy)	(wages, class size, grievance process, right to bargain)	(through third-party intervention, agreement, or injunction)

↘ Strike ↗

Each of these steps presents research problems, as the studies summarized on the preceding pages show. Bruno and Nelken (1975) studied very few teachers, none of whom had ever struck, in a single county; Nasstrom and Brelsford (1976) found that their data contradicted the Bruno-Nelken conclusions in some cases. Thus, knowing the characteristics of teachers does not seem very useful, all things considered, in predicting strike behavior.

Studies of the effect of organizational structure on strikes are not applicable to the NEA and AFT, since local associations of teachers do not need the approval of the national leadership to go on strike. Impasse issues are, to me, the most suspect of all explanatory variables in this model. During collective bargaining, both parties give and take on numerous issues, making it difficult to pinpoint exactly which issue stopped the bargaining. Also, it may be difficult to separate out what is a wage issue and what is not, since almost all economic benefits can be figured in financial terms. Finally, in bargaining, what happens if a number of issues create blockages? Such multi-issue situations are confused in the research done to date.

Analyses of case studies of key strikes indicate still another shortcoming of current research on strike causes: Strikes can occur for reasons unrelated to bargaining. In labor relations, disputes also arise in the implementation of contracts, when grievance procedures break down, and when unions perceive threats to their existence from outside the school organization. The prototypical case was the series of walkouts in New York City between 1960 and 1969, not one of which occurred during bargaining. In November 1960, a new coalition of teachers, the United Federation of Teachers (UFT), called a one-day strike to "demand a collective-bargaining election" and the right to unionize (Ravitch 1974, p. 264). It worked; an election was held, the UFT won, and the board of education duly recognized the federation as the bargaining agent for teachers.

The second and third strikes were likewise unrelated to the breakdown in bargaining and impasse. Rather, these stoppages were union responses to perceived threats to teachers from community groups, in the Ocean Hill-Brownsville section of Brooklyn, P.S. 201 in Harlem, and elsewhere. Although the issues were far too complex to enumerate here, it can be concluded that power, not a bargaining or impasse dilemma, was the stimulus for the walkouts. Ravitch (1974) explains:

> The day before school was to open, September 8, Mayor Lindsay announced that a strike had been averted and that Ocean Hill-Brownsville would not prevent the return of the UFT teachers. However, McCoy [leader of the black-dominated local school district] stated publicly that the UFT teachers would not resume their normal duties, but would be reassigned within the district. It was no longer a question of the ten who had been dismissed originally, but of the district's other UFT teachers who had been replaced by new teachers. Reassignment was not acceptable to the union; Shanker [UFT president] declared that school would not open on September 9 (p. 366).

The third strike in New York City also revolved around the UFT's reaction to the power of the community organization in Ocean Hill-Brownsville; the community leadership refused the requests of the union that all hiring and firing of staff be conducted with due process. Strike leader Albert Shanker, in an undated letter to the membership, expressed the UFT's position:

> We wanted to wait, but we could have done so only on the basis of concrete action, because we've had too many empty words and promises. They [Board promises] held up no better than the written agreements that the Board of Education, the Superintendent, and the Mayor find so simple to violate. If it becomes necessary to close down Ocean Hill-Brownsville . . . because of its refusal to abide by decency and due process, we stand ready to turn to any community in the city that wants to conduct an honest experiment in innovation . . . [but] on only the minimum basis that due process, free speech, and academic freedom will be maintained. . . . The issue is what it has been all along—will we have a school system in which justice, due process and dignity for teachers is possible, or will we have a system in which any group of vigilantes can enter a school and take it over with intimidation and threats of violence. . . . This may be a long one—for this time we are staying out and not going back until we are sure we still have a school system in the City of New York.

Narrowly defined, the cause of these strikes was a violation of the due process procedures through which teachers and school administrators, who also went on strike under the leadership of the Council of Supervisory Associations (CSA), were transferred without "just cause." From the perspective of the UFT and CSA, their contracts were violated. But, in reality, the strike was conducted to assert the power of the administrator and teacher groups over their occupational lives.

Summary

Educator strikes appear to be both rational and irrational. True, there is often a breakdown in the bilateral processes of bargaining, grieving, and executing the contract. Certain kinds of teachers appear to have higher propensities to walk out, at least as they themselves report their likely actions, just as certain industries have more strikes than others, perhaps because of their structure. Workers make the rational choice to leave their jobs when other courses of action, such as negotiations and third-party interventions, have been exhausted. But, at the point of voting to strike, employees in the public sector, often knowing they are breaking the law, act with some emotion. Pride and anger are involved—emotions that cannot be captured in survey research.

We need, then, studies of the group psychology of strikes—the motivations, feelings, and actions behind them. Do strikers as a group have emotions similar to those of soldiers preparing for battle, revolutionaries planning a coup, or athletes before a game? Furthermore, what happens before, during, and after a strike? How do various subgroups, such as the black teachers in Ocean Hill-Brownsville, feel about strikes? How are strike coalitions built and maintained? How are strikes broken by management? How do the causes behind strikes lose their salience to reasons for returning to work?

Costs of Collective Bargaining in Education

It has been widely believed that collective bargaining and the power to strike radically altered the financing of schools. Once teachers gained greater control, they made such demands on taxpayers that the expenses for public schools skyrocketed. This section tests these assumptions. Specifically, it weighs the research findings on the following questions:

1. Does teacher bargaining drive up the absolute wage costs? If so, by how much?
2. Is there evidence of "spillover," whereby nonbargaining school systems in proximity to unionized ones react by raising their wages and fringe benefits to compete?
3. Are there special teacher subgroups (for instance, high or low on the salary schedule) that benefit more than others from collective bargaining? Put differently, does bargaining affect the structure of teacher wages?
4. Are funds diverted from programs, materials, and facilities to pay the wages of unionized teachers?

The literature on these topics is more extensive and quantitative than the studies of reasons for bargaining and the rationale for strikes. Perhaps this is so because one can measure an increase in a district's average salary more easily than a supposed or hypothesized shift in staff attitudes or beliefs that might lead to collective bargaining or a labor walkout. Also, not surprisingly, analysts in the area of labor relations generally come from a finance or economics background; the sharing of a common language among these scholars promotes an interaction of ideas and, accordingly, more extensive analysis.

Bargaining and Absolute Increases in Teacher Salaries

Although the discipline of economics and finance share a common perspective, this similarity does not guarantee consensus in the results of interpretation. The question, To what extent does bargaining raise the salaries of teachers in absolute terms? has not received a single answer in the research of the past seven or eight years. Most scholars have concluded that bargaining only raises pay slightly; see Lewin (1977) for a comprehensive treatment of the research. In spite of the difficulty of separating the general upward drift of salaries for teachers (which had so long been depressed) from the impact of unionization, what does seem obvious is that bargaining has *not* led to the enormous increases in pay that were predicted.

Robert E. Doherty (1980), in his extensive review of teacher bargaining for the Industrial Relations Research Association, states: "Per pupil costs in adjusted 1973-74 dollars rose from slightly less than $250 annually in 1930 to more than $1,200 in 1974, *a 380 percent increase*." He concludes that, although educational costs have soared over a forty-year period, the impact of bargaining on wages has been "modest" (pp. 492-93, 542).

> Studies that have tried to determine the effect of collective bargaining on salaries and other conditions of employment suggest that bargaining has resulted in modest gains for teachers, from approximately 1 to 5 percent in the overall, with the most significant gains being realized by those with several years' experience and large numbers of graduate credits (p. 542).

Doherty's conclusions were based on his assessment of the research of others, not his own. My own review of the literature on this subject, discussed below, tends to support his statement that bargaining has had only a minor impact on the wages of teachers and other employees.

Perry's (1979) indepth study of nine school districts, an updating of some of his earlier research (see Perry and Wildman 1970), supports what others have found through larger-scale studies:

> Collective bargaining in these [nine] systems has continued to add varying amounts to the total cost of salary settlements, but the cumulative effect of these increases on average teacher salary, overall budget size, and percent of budget devoted to teacher salaries has not been substantial in aggregate terms (p. 12).

Further, when comparing data from his microanalysis to wider, private-sector results, he concluded that "collective bargaining in public education has not produced dramatically different results than it has in the private sector" (p. 12).

Perhaps the most comprehensive study of the impact of collective bargaining on teachers' salaries was conducted by Lipsky and Drotning (1973). These scholars analyzed data from 696 school districts in New York State one year after passage of the Taylor Law (1962), which authorized collective bargaining in that state for the first time. The timing of the study was ideal for making a sample before-and-after comparison between districts that participated in collective negotiations (63 percent of the sample 696 districts) and districts that did not.

To provide a representative view of the entire salary structure, the study considered compensation at three points along the salary scale: (1) first-year teachers with only a bachelor's degree; (2) teachers with a B.A., seven years of experience, and sixty hours of earned graduate credit; and (3) teachers with a B.A., eleven years of experience, and sixty hours of earned graduate credit. This three-tiered analysis format seems preferable to that of other studies, which have relied solely on base salary as a measurement (see, for example, Baird and Landon 1972). Lipsky and Drotning point out the difficulty in the base-salary-only approach:

> A district can adjust a schedule to show, for example, relatively high salaries at the base level but relatively low salaries at subsequent steps. If the district's teachers are employed mainly at the higher

steps and no hiring is being done, the average salary actually paid by the district will tend to be lower than other districts with, possibly, a lower base salary but a different age-distribution of teachers. Thus, the common practice of using the base salary as a comprehensive index of a district's average salary level can be quite misleading. Both administrators and teacher organizations can manipulate the salary schedule to serve various purposes—public relations, politics, recruiting, etc. (p. 23).

Analyzing these three salary points, Lipsky and Drotning found only a modest relationship between bargaining and teacher salaries:

There were indeed differences in salaries at all levels between districts with and without contracts. This, however, does not take us very far. First, the salary differences between districts are not very large: from about one percent ($65) at base to 2.24 percent ($240) at the BS + 60, 11th Step. Second, of course, we are not controlling for any other variables influencing teacher salaries (p. 20).

Among the other variables that might be used to explain the differential between bargaining and nonbargaining districts, Lipsky and Drotning considered the desirability of a district (by looking at size and student/teacher ratios), the ability of each district to meet salary demands, the monopsony power of each district (competitiveness), and the height of salary level prior to collective bargaining. This last variable alone explained almost 50 percent of the differential originally reported. Organized districts that paid $65-$240 more than nonbargaining districts in 1968 had, in fact, paid $25-$125 more in the year prior to passage of the Taylor Law. On balance, the authors drew the conclusion that "collective bargaining . . . had no effect on teacher salary levels, regardless of whether the dependent variable was a measure of actual earnings (mean salary) or of scheduled rates" (p. 35).

A similar study by Rehmus and Wilner (1965) in Michigan produced very different, and somewhat suspect, findings. Unlike Lipsky and Drotning, who examined both bargaining and nonbargaining districts before and after passage of the public employment relations law in New York, Rehmus and Wilner examined only districts (twelve in all) that had contracts. In those twelve districts as a whole, Rehmus and Wilner found that salaries for teachers with bachelor's degrees rose at a rate of 2.8 percent in 1961, before collective bargaining was authorized. In 1968, after bargaining, the rate of increase was 8.5 percent. For teachers with master's degrees, the respective rates of salary increase were 3.5 percent and 10.5 percent. The authors observed that the rate of salary increases had nearly tripled, and they attributed the change to collective bargaining.

As Thornton (1970) points out, the Rehmus-Wilner study is riddled with problems: first, they provide no comparative data for Michigan districts that were not bargaining. Second, Thornton found that two of the twelve systems had actually been bargaining prior to 1967-68, thus contaminating the pre-/post nature of their study. Third, it is unclear why Rehmus and Wilner selected these twelve districts and not others—suggesting the existence of an unknown bias in the study. And, fourth, a sample of 12 out of 148 Michigan districts is hardly significant. Moreover, when Thornton analyzed teacher salary gains over the same time period in Arkansas, a state with no collective bargaining, he found salary increases of similar magnitude to those in the twelve bargaining districts in Michigan. Using data from the United States Bureau of Labor Statistics, Thornton concluded that teacher shortages were a more likely explanation than collective bargaining for the salary increases reported (p. 38).

In an attempt to correct for these methodological problems, Thornton limited his sample to eighty-three urban school districts in United States cities with populations of at least 100,000. Thornton chose large urban districts in the belief that effective bargaining was more likely to occur in these districts; he also desired a standardized microlevel sample to avoid the statistical distortions of more aggregated data compiled across districts of varying size and type. The study controlled for the independent variables by measuring (1) the percentage of fulltime classroom teachers with less than standard teaching certificates (as a measure of demand for teachers), (2) the presence of a collectively negotiated contract in the previous year as a measure of the level of negotiating strength in each district, and (3) the level of wages and salaries in the city or surrounding county (as a measure of wage spillover from other occupations that would tend to pull

87

up teacher salaries). For his dependent variables, Thornton tested wages at four points along the salary scale: both minimum and maximum salary levels for teachers holding bachelor's degrees and those holding master's.

Thornton's multiple regression analysis revealed that "collective negotiations have indeed affected higher teachers' salaries at all four salary levels. The differentials range from a fairly small $160 for the A.M. [master's degree] minimum to a substantial $3,132 at the A.M. maximum level [2.8 and 28.8 percent respectively]" (pp. 42-43). Thornton checked the veracity of these differentials by examining salary differences between the negotiating and nonnegotiating districts ten years earlier. The results, displayed in table 9, confirm the findings of Lipsky and Drotning (1973). Thornton discovered that salary levels prior to unionization were a partial but not complete explanation of the salary differential between negotiating and nonnegotiating districts.

Table 9

Percentage Differences in Salary Levels,[a]
Negotiating vs. Nonnegotiating Districts 1969-70 and 1958-59

Salary Level	Percentage 1969-70	1958-59
A.B. minimum	3.7	0.0
A.B. maximum	5.0	3.9
A.M. minimum	2.3	-1.6
A.M. maximum	28.8	5.9

[a]Partial regression coefficients as a percentage of mean salaries in nonnegotiating districts. Source: Thornton (1970), p. 43.

In short, not all of the observed 1969 differences can be reasonably attributed to collective negotiations on the part of teachers. Negotiating districts appear to have succeeded instead in widening already existing percentage salary differentials. Assuming that the 1969 and 1958 percentage estimates differ significantly at each salary level, it might be concluded that the extent to which teachers' bargaining has raised relative salaries ranges from about 1 percent to 4 percent at the three lower salary levels to nearly 23 percent at the A.M. maximum level (pp. 44-45).

Thornton admits, however, that the "surprisingly high A.M. maximum figure is subject to some degree of reservation." Although Thornton improved on the research of his predecessors, the reliability of his results, especially the 23 percent differential at the A.M. maximum level, is open to question. Most researchers in the field agree that microlevel samples are preferable to larger aggregations, but Hall and Carroll (1973) find difficulties in Thornton's (1970) interstate comparison of large districts:

> The first problem stems from the districts included in the sample. In both studies [Baird and Landon's 1972 study is also criticized], the samples were interstate and interregional in nature. As a result, it is not clear whether their findings reflected the impact of unions on salaries or whether they attributed the influence of variables such as state certification requirements, degree of urbanization, and regional income differentials to teachers' organizations (p. 835).

The impact of this indictment is difficult to gauge. Thornton seems to have controlled partially for the degree of urbanization by measuring the wage rates of other occupations in the surrounding county, but the significance and direction of bias from state certification requirements and regional income differentials are uncertain. Nevertheless, Thornton's consideration of salary levels from two different time frames ten years apart would seem to account at least partially for these variables, and his close replication of results found by other studies should give us a fair degree of confidence in the accuracy of his conclusions.

Like economists before them, Baird and Landon (1972) were highly critical of previous studies and sought to improve on the models used in them. Baird and Landon employed multiple-regression equations similar to those used by Kasper (1973) and Thornton (1970), controlling for the independent variables that measured relative wealth of districts, the structure of the labor market, and the degree of teacher organization. Using base salary as the dependent variable, the analysts surveyed forty-four school districts with enrollments of from 25,000 to 50,000 and concluded: "In districts where some type of collective negotiations are held, salaries tend to be significantly higher—by an average of $261.17 or 4.9% of the average starting salary" (p. 415).

Despite their efforts to improve on the research of others, two methodological problems damage the credibility of Baird and Landon's results. First, and most important, the authors do not control for salary levels prior to bargaining; hence their results would tend to be overestimated, because much of the differential between organized and unorganized districts can be explained by salary differences before unionization, as Thornton (1970) and Lipsky and Drotning (1973) have demonstrated. Finally, Baird and Landon's use of base salary, rather than the mean salary level or several points along the salary scale, as their dependent variable is questionable. Lipsky and Drotning have demonstrated the unreliability of this measure, and Kasper (1973) has raised a further question about the appropriateness of using the base salary as the dependent variable:

> The point here is whether one can correlate starting salaries with negotiations in the absence of any logical discussion of the possible effect of the latter on the former. Why should current union members devote any time or economic resources to raising the wages of unknown persons who may become members next year, that is, starting teachers? (p. 420)

While union members might contest the assertion that they fight for existing members, not potential ones, the fact remains: the use of base or new-teacher salaries, rather than a range of points on the salary schedule, and the absence of data prior to bargaining flaw Baird and Landon's study.

Frey (1975) built a model of salary decisions in public education, one that accounted for both endogenous and exogenous variables in a single state (New Jersey). Central to Frey's theory was a view that collective bargaining is "a process whereby wage variables that were once unilaterally determined by a school board are jointly·determined by the school board and the teachers' association" (p. 195). Using data from 298 districts over a six-year period, he tested his model and found the following.

First, wealth of communities, a key exogenous variable, accounted for very few of the salary differentials among school systems. Why? Perhaps, as Frey theorizes, "wealthy school systems may not greatly outbid poorer school districts for more capable teachers"—they may not have to, since richer systems may be "more pleasant places in which to work" (p. 217). But why could not richer districts hold their salaries below those of poor systems and depend on the amenities of their upper-class schools to attract good teachers for less pay (as indeed some of the more prestigious private schools and colleges seem to do)? Although Frey does not know the answer, he speculates that perhaps the pressures of district wealth (which tend to inflate teacher wages) may be counteracted by the amenities (which may press to reduce pay increases). But such precise cancelling is unlikely, Frey concedes.

Second, district size "has a very small impact on teachers' wages," a finding accounted for by the fact that teachers have divergent views on the size of school districts in which they prefer to work (p. 218). Third, Frey found that "alternative wage" is the major determinant of teacher wages; that is, teacher pay increases are roughly comparable to those of equivalent occupations in the general society. Frey predicts, in fact, "that teachers' wages will continue to rise at a rapid rate as long as general wage inflation is rapid" and that educational expenses will continue to increase (p. 219). It is interesting to note that his prediction has not come about, in part because of the cutbacks in public spending, declining enrollments, and the widening gap between general private-sector wage increases and those for public school teachers. Teachers' real wages have dropped significantly as the job market for certified teachers moved from one of scarcity to one of surplus. In effect, the Frey equilibrium model requires retesting in a market where there are many more teachers than jobs.

Finally, Frey found, as have others, that "collective bargaining seems to have a very small impact on teachers' wages" (p. 219). Except for the few unique situations in large cities (see Schmenner 1973) at the very onset of collective bargaining, when teachers' wages were very low and their political power was on the rise, bargaining does not seem to be a significant cause of teacher wage increases.

The work of Kasper (1970) has probably generated more

scholarly debate than any other study on this issue. Kasper analyzed Illinois data from the 1967-68 school year and used the degree of bargaining as his primary control. He concludes:

> For the time being, all that may be said is (1) collective representation does not seem to have had much, if any, effect on teachers' salaries; (2) if there has been a positive effect, it is probably less than $400 and could even be as little as $40; (3) given these small estimates, it seems unlikely that bargaining has produced a significant or widespread reallocation of educational resources (p. 71).

Kasper offers five possible reasons why collective bargaining may have little impact on teacher salaries:

> First, it may be much more difficult for public officials to raise the prices of their "products" than for private firms, since the former may have to go to the taxpayers for an all-or-nothing tax levy or bond issue to pay for higher employee costs. Second, depending on the product, it may be more difficult for public than private managers to reduce the quantity or lower the quality of services. Third, if a community accepts historical occupational differentials among public employees, an increase in the salaries of one group could be expected to lead to large budgetary outlays for all groups combined, i.e., wage "spillover" may be at least as important in the public as private sector. Fourth, unionization may be viewed as an unnecessary attack from unappreciative teachers on the amateur policy-making school board members and on the community at large. Fifth, the traditions of "professionalization" and "community interest" may still militate against the full and effective use of bargaining power by teachers (p. 60).

Kasper's conclusions seem to contradict the results of other studies (see Shapiro 1978), and he is criticized by a parade of doubters including Hall and Carroll (1973), Thornton (1970), and particularly Baird and Landon (1972). Although criticisms are numerous, the chief complaint concerns Kasper's reliance on statewide data instead of data from the district level where collective bargaining actually occurs. Kasper (1973) concedes that microlevel data are generally preferable but defends the use of aggregated data because of the growing role of the state in education. State regulation of pension programs and teacher certification, according to Kasper, are factors that provide some degree of standardization within the state and make states a reliable testing ground (p. 419).

This methodological dispute is not nearly as important as

the literature would suggest, because, when Kasper reanalyzed his data three years later in response to criticism from Baird and Landon, his results were remarkably close to those of his critics. He wrote:

> Initially, I examined a variety of one-equation models and found that in general the extent of organization had no statistically significant effect on teachers' salaries. However, the "more appropriate" simultaneous models, estimated by two-stage least-squares regressions, did produce statistically significant coefficients. From the parameter estimates of the latter models, I drew the inference that "the extent of organization . . . tended to raise salaries by no more than 4 percent (or nearly $275) across the board," which, I said, seemed "like much hard work for little financial return."
>
> Thus, for practical purposes, our numerical estimates may be identical: I find "little if any" effect, 4.9 percent perhaps; they find "substantial positive influence," 4.9 percent. Teachers will be less inclined to quibble about this difference than economists (1973, p. 418).

Given the wide range of methodologies utilized by researchers in this field, and the amount of ink devoted to criticism of previous research, it is truly remarkable that the studies reviewed are in such close agreement. Taken as a whole, the research suggests that the influence of collective bargaining in education increases teacher salaries from about 5 to 9 percent higher than they would be otherwise. Compared to wage gains won by unionized noneducation public employees—estimated by Ehrenberg (1973) to be 12 to 16 percent larger than those of nonorganized employees—the increases won by teacher unions may seem paltry. Yet, when we consider factors beyond absolute salary increases, including spillover, pension, and antidiscrimination benefits, the impact of collective bargaining in education attains greater significance.

Spillover Benefits

Kasper (1970) refers in passing to an important concept that the research has treated only tangentially—the concept of spillover. There is some indication that wages in school districts without union activity have increased at a comparable rate to wages in bargaining districts. It would thus seem that a "spillover" of union-won benefits is affecting nonunionized areas. Lipsky and Drotning (1973) provide two hypotheses for this spillover: (1) The nonbargaining district may simply want to protect its position as a competitive employer in the job market and retain quality teachers; (2) school managers may wish to appease teachers with wage increases, thus defusing union activity in their own districts and avoiding the loss of management prerogatives to unionized teachers (p. 29).

Ehrenberg (1973) designed a study of unionized, noneducation, public-sector employees to measure the spillover effect. Analyzing data from ten categories of employees in 478 cities, he estimated the effects of unionization at three different levels of government (municipal, county, and SMSA) to control for spillover. He concluded:

> The geographic wage spillovers tended to be primarily unidirectional with the suburban category wage influencing the central city category wage more often than the reverse occurred. On average, because of the extent of organization of central city municipal employees, wages of suburban government employees were estimated by us to be 4% higher in 1967 than they would have been in the absence of central city unions. Similarly, due to the extent of organization of suburban government employees, central city municipal employees' wages were about 4.4% higher on average in 1967 than they would have been in the absence of suburban unions (p. 151).

The significance of this indirect impact of collective bargaining should be clear. According to Ehrenberg, "these 'spillover' results suggest that merely focusing attention on estimated union/nonunion wage differentials will lead to an *underestimate* of the impact of municipal employee unions on public sector wages" (p. 151).

Hall and Carroll (1973) confirm that what Ehrenberg has outlined for noneducation public employees is equally true for teachers. Their research (which will be reviewed more extensively at the end of this section) revealed that bargaining units increased teacher salaries in suburban areas by an average of $165 per year—a figure they report to be in line with the estimates of Kasper (1970) and Baird and Landon (1972). The authors, however, qualify this seemingly modest effect:

Lest supporters of collective negotiations despair over the size of measured salary effects of formal contracts, it should be pointed out that our estimates may well understate the total influence of teachers' organizations on teacher pay. There is some evidence that unorganized districts have raised pay in response to higher salaries in neighboring areas or have increased salaries to discourage teacher militancy. The size of these "spillover" benefits is unknown. In our sample, since only one-third of the districts had contracts, they may be relatively small. Nevertheless, "spillover" effects combined with the direct impact may make the total effect somewhat more substantial (p. 841).

Kasper (1970) and Lipsky and Drotning (1973) have attempted to estimate the "unknown" influence of spillover. Although Kasper did not provide a detailed methodology in his published reply of 1973, he projected that, controlling for spillover, union representation may have raised teacher salaries by as much as 6.7 percent in Ohio (p. 423).

The New York State data in the Lipsky and Drotning study provided an ideal opportunity to control for the influence of spillover, as the authors explain:

> A district that is isolated geographically will be relatively immune to pattern effects. The experience of the parties in negotiations provides some prima facie evidence to support this assumption: when comparisons are used as a standard for salary determination, it is inevitably nearby or adjacent districts that are used for the purpose. The more distant the district, the less relevance it has for the parties. . . . If a subsample consisting of relatively isolated districts can be selected, the influence of spillover will be reduced, if not eliminated. Furthermore, such a sample would consist of districts operating in less competitive, more monopsonistic labor markets. For example, a sample might be constructed consisting only of small-town districts or districts within a given enrollment range—that is, those relatively uninfluenced by geographically proximate districts and therefore less involved in any orbit of coercive comparison" (p. 29).

Lipsky and Drotning selected a subsample of eighty-eight districts in the state with enrollments of between 1,000 and 2,000 pupils. About 63 percent of these districts were organized, a figure that coincides with the statewide average. Running this sample through their multiple-regression equations, the authors found that collective bargaining was associated with a $72 increase in base salaries and a $313 increase in BS + 60 (11th step) salaries. Percentage increases at four different salary levels are shown in table 10.

Collective Bargaining

Table 10

Percentage Increases in Teacher Salaries in a Subsample of School Districts in New York State

Salary Level	Percentage
Base salary	1.12
BS + 30, 7th Step	2.15
BS + 60, 11th Step	2.95
Mean salary	2.41

Source: Lipsky and Drotning 1973.

Comparison of this subsample to the statewide data confirms the hypothesis that spillover effects tend to mask the impact of collective bargaining in education. This comparison is shown in table 11.

Table 11

Difference in Salary Levels between New York State School Districts with and without Collective Bargaining Contracts, 1968-69

Salary Level	Union Districts with Contracts (N=441) Mean (1)	Standard Deviation (2)	Nonunion Districts without Contracts (N=255) Mean (3)	Standard Deviation (4)	Percentage Difference (1)-(3)÷(3) (5)
Base salary	$ 6,485	$ 275.9	6,420	$ 299.1	1.01
BS + 30, 7th Step	9,091	615.8	8,943	652.0	1.65
BS + 60, 11th Step	10,931	1,166.0	10,691	1,016.5	2.21
Mean salary	8,539	1,093.6	8,385	1,190.4	1.84

Source: Lipsky and Drotning 1973.

Salary schedules in adjacent school districts, then, do have an effect on each other, an effect union activity may magnify. As Baird and Landon (1972) note, this relationship is benefi-

cial to both sides of the union fence:
> While teachers do benefit from unionization, they are the losers when school districts are consolidated. The ability to play one school district against another benefits unionized as well as unorganized teachers (p. 417).

Baird and Landon estimate that "a doubling of the number of districts in the area would be associated with an increase in the beginning salary of about $164.38" (p. 416). Deconsolidation would therefore seem to benefit teachers.

Nonsalary Benefits for Teachers

When the effect of unionization on nonsalary benefits is added to spillover effects, the total influence of collective bargaining in education grows in significance. Gallagher (1978) notes that the research generally ignores such nonsalary compensation areas as pension plans, insurance, and health care programs, and it also excludes union efforts to improve working conditions by limiting class size, hiring teaching aides, providing duty-free lunch periods, and reducing teaching load.

In his study of 133 public school districts in Illinois with average daily attendance (ADA) levels of between 500 and 4,000, Gallagher sought to examine the relationship of unionization to increase in nonsalary compensation. He compared sixty-eight nonbargaining districts to sixty-five bargaining districts, controlling for school district wealth and for the percentage of certified staff with advanced degrees. The multiple regression analysis indicated that collective bargaining districts spent $87 more per ADA in total operating expenditures than nonbargaining districts, $52 of which went for certified staff salaries and $35 for expenditures not related to teacher compensation (p. 234). These differences represent an advantage of approximately 9 percent for bargaining districts over nonbargaining districts. Gallagher concludes:
> In view of the results presented here and those of past teacher salary determination studies, it appears that this significant relationship between collective bargaining and total district per ADA expenditures for certified teacher salaries may be partly due to a significant

relationship between collective bargaining and annual teacher salary levels. However, nondirect conpensation gains made by the certified instructional staff through bargaining may also be influential. Realized bargaining gains such as extended sick leave, personal days off, sabbatical leave, and other compensated leave provisions may contribute to higher total salary expenditures by requiring the district to secure and compensate additional temporary or substitute teaching staff as replacements while the regular teaching staff utilizes their leave provisions. In addition, it is probable that increased total district expenditures for teacher salary compensation on a per ADA basis may be due in part to higher unit (ADA) costs imposed by contractual limitations on class size and limitations on staff reductions resulting from the collective bargaining process. . . .

Collective bargaining is significantly and positively related to total nonteacher salary related expenditures, but this significant relationship appears largely attributable to a possible "spillover" effect which collective bargaining may have on salary expenditures for other school district personnel, in particular, principals, assistant principals, and operation and maintenance employees, as well as the possible significant effect which collective bargaining may have on staff insurance and retirement programs (p. 236).

The spillover salary benefits to nonteaching instructional staff should not be confused with spillover benefits accruing to teachers in nonunionized school districts. In the former case, the spillover effect occurs within the same school district, where administrators and support staff have their salaries pulled up by the successful negotiations of teacher unions.

Although Gallagher does demonstrate the significance of nonsalary benefits won by unions, the observed difference between bargaining and nonbargaining districts may be inflated by the study's failure to control for differentials that may have existed prior to collective bargaining, as Thornton (1970) and Lipsky and Drotning (1973) have shown. This problem, however, does not seriously damage Gallagher's conclusion. Although the total differential between bargaining and nonbargaining districts may be inflated, the important finding is not the total amount of the gap but the net difference between teacher salary gains and total expenditure increases for the bargaining district. The $35 per ADA increase in nonteacher expenditures over and above the teacher salary gains won by unions supports the hypothesis that, when nonsalary benefits are considered, the significance attributed to collective bargaining in education vastly increases.

Gustman and Segal's (1977) analysis of interstate variations in teacher pensions lends further support to Gallagher's findings. Gustman and Segal are economists who rely on statewide aggregated data for their interstate comparisons; they contend that the determination of pension benefits by state legislatures rather than by local school districts makes this aggregation appropriate. Controlling for the availability of Social Security payments and average teacher salaries, the authors found that

> in states with a 100 percent coverage by negotiated agreements, pensions paid after 25 years of service would be 54 percent greater than pensions from states with no such coverage. In our sample, coverage ranged from 0 to 88 percent of the teachers in a given state; thus, the maximum difference in pensions attributable to the effect of teacher organizations is about 48 percent (p. 341).

Gustman and Segal calculated that the net effect of teacher unions on pensions is approximately the same as their effect on salaries.

> Our results suggest that in the extreme case, where teachers are fully covered by negotiated agreements, current pension costs might be raised to 15 percent of salary—i.e., the effect of teacher organizations may be to increase benefits by an amount equal to 5 percent of salary. Such an increase corresponds roughly to what has been estimated as the effect of teacher unions on salaries themselves (p. 342).

Special Constituencies

Are teacher unions egalitarian? Do their victories benefit teachers from groups that have endured discrimination? Traditionally in education, both women and elementary school teachers (two groups that often overlap) have been paid lower wages than men for the same type of work.

Holmes (1979) surveyed data from 456 independent school districts in the state of Oklahoma during the 1974-75 school year to determine if these two special constituencies were benefited by collective bargaining. The study controlled for the level of union activity (from low union activity [UA = 0] to high [UA = 4]), district wealth, and urban location. Some of Holmes's results are presented in table 12. He notes that his results are consistent with previous research that measured the influence of unions in the private sector. He reports that

> it is clear that union activity has had a significant impact on the structure of teachers' earnings. The results of the interaction between union activity and the earnings differential between male and female and elementary and secondary teachers tentatively support the hypothesis that increased activity reduces these differentials. In school districts with no union activity, males received a premium of $610, while in districts with the most advanced level of union activity this premium was only $436. This difference is statistically significant at the 99 percent level. Further, with the exception of districts with union activity level three, there is a decline in the premium as the level of activity increases. The same general trend is observed in the premium paid secondary teachers relative to elementary teachers, with significant declines in the premium for each increasing step in union activity from level one through level four. . . . The results for teachers in districts with no union activity do not, however, conform to the hypothesis. Nevertheless, as an overall conclusion it can be stated that increasing levels of union activity do tend to narrow the differential wages between male and female and elementary and secondary teachers as hypothesized (pp. 82-83).

Table 12

Comparison of Male and Female
Elementary and Secondary Teacher Salaries
by Level of Union Activity (UA)*

Level of union activity	White male Elementary	White male Secondary	White female Elementary	White female Secondary
UA=0	$8560	$ 8976	$7959	$8195
UA=1	9275	9653	8674	9052
UA=2	9485	9835	9055	9405
UA=3	8581	8925	7970	8314
UA=4	9924	10,257	9489	9822

*Where coefficients for a particular characteristic were not significantly different for different levels of union activity the average was used.
Source: Holmes 1979.

The only incongruity in the results occurs at level three of union activity (moderately high). Holmes theorizes that better measures of union activity may be needed to explain this anomaly and suggests that future research should address the existence of a threshold for effective union activity. Doherty (1980) found that bargaining aided those at the upper end of the salary schedule, since school boards and teacher unions tended to bargain ratio-percentage raises. Further, with the significant drop in teacher turnover, the faculties of many districts become "older" and exert pressure to receive larger increments than those received by the few newer staffers.

In summary, collective bargaining has helped to narrow differences in pay levels between women and men and between elementary and secondary staff and has also brought relatively greater pay increases to teachers at the higher levels of the salary schedule.

Rate of Salary Increases

All the research reviewed thus far demonstrates that collective bargaining has had a moderate influence on the increase in teacher salaries. Union and nonunion gains in the areas of spillover, nonteacher expenditures, improved working conditions, and benefits to special constituency groups are additive in their impact. Collective bargaining does not seem to reverse wage trends in nonunionized districts; instead, the bargaining process accelerates the acquisition of benefits that nonunionized teachers would otherwise receive over time.

Lipsky and Drotning (1973) suggest that measuring the rate of salary increases will shed more light on the nature of bargaining gains in public education than measuring absolute increases. When analyzed in this fashion, the impact of collective bargaining gains new importance. The results of these authors' comparison of changes in salary levels in New York school districts with and without collective bargaining contracts are shown in table 13. Lipsky and Drotning explain:

> The results indicate that the presence of a contract added about $83 to the amount by which base salary was increased from 1967 to 1968. The corresponding figures are $110 at the BS + 30, 7th Step and $131 at the BS + 60, 11th Step. Thus, the collective bargaining apparently resulted in salary increases that were approximately 15 percent greater than one would have expected otherwise (p. 32).

Table 13

Changes in Salary Levels, 1967-68: Differences between New York School Districts with and without Collective Bargaining Contracts

Salary Level	Districts with Contracts (N=441) Mean	Standard Deviation	Districts without Contracts (N=225) Mean	Standard Deviation
Base Salary	$598	$211.7	$558	$293.4
BS + 30, 7th Step	782	297.6	704	402.2
BS + 60, 11th Step	986	410.2	871	521.0

Source: Lipsky and Drotning 1973.

Structural Effects

Up to this point, our review has concentrated primarily on the influence of collective bargaining on the level of salary and nonsalary benefits to teachers. But what are the structural effects of collective bargaining? Who gains most from union activity—experienced teachers at the upper end of the salary scale or relatively new union members?

The results of studies that have touched on this issue are mixed (see Thornton 1970 and Doherty 1980, pp. 542 ff). Concerning pension benefits, Gustman and Segal (1977) have pointed out that teachers with modest pensions are relative winners, but, in the area of teacher salaries, Kasper (1970) and Thornton (1970) have shown that teachers on the upper end of the career ladder are relatively advantaged. To further complicate the issue, Holmes (1979) has found that salary increases resulting from collective bargaining have the ancillary effect of closing the wage gap between male and female and elementary and secondary teachers.

A later study by Gustman and Segal (1977) specifically analyzed changes in teacher salary structures brought about by collective bargaining. Controlling for the influence of the surrounding labor market and the level of bargaining activity, the study analyzed data from ninety-three central-city school districts. Gustman and Segal hypothesized that calling for changes in salary structure might be a more appealing political route for unions to take, for two reasons:

> First, while such a policy is flexible in that it can be shaped to benefit almost as many members of the union as would a general salary increase, its cost implications are not as easily perceived or understood by a public that may potentially exert political pressure and stiffen the resistance of elected officials to union demands. Second, a change in salary structure can be used to bring greatest relative gains to those groups that wield the greatest political power in the union (p. 437).

Gustman and Segal found that "collective bargaining has had no significant impact on *starting* salaries." They noted that "the reason for this may be the high visibility of increases in the basic salary."

> It appears that in unionized areas the number of steps in both educational tracks has been reduced relative to nonunion areas by 1½-2½ steps. . . . Our findings also indicate that by raising the maximum salary, comprehensive agreements increase the difference between the starting and the maximum salaries in the M.A. track, (MA+) - (MA-), by about $600.
> . . . the effect of reducing the number of steps by one on next year's earnings increases linearly according to the teachers' experience up to a level two steps below the highest. For a teacher now at that level, next year's increase is doubled up (pp. 439 and 443).

It is difficult to draw general conclusions from Gustman and Segal's findings, other than the fact additional research is clearly needed. Helping to put the findings into a broader, albeit union, perspective is a comment by Richard Prosten (1978) of the AFL-CIO:

> We conclude from the Gustman/Segal paper that collective bargaining agents representing teachers have performed admirably, at least in terms of fulfilling the desires of their members. The authors suggest that unions may attempt to mask some of the cost implications of their wage demands by restructuring salary schedules rather than accepting general wage increases, and that they may seek those changes which will most benefit those union members "that wield greatest political power"—whatever that means. While it is not clear to me that they have proved the latter assertion, they have concluded that experienced teachers covered by what they call "comprehensive agreements" have been financially served by the collective bargaining

process. One would have to conclude from this paper that experience and seniority are not generally rewarded by school systems without substantial prodding (p. 446).

Who Pays?

From the research under review, it is clear that collective bargaining in education has had the effect of raising costs for school district managers. Gallagher (1978) estimates that union activity increases the total budget of a school district by approximately 9 percent (p. 234), but where does this extra money come from?

Gallagher contends that nonsalary areas of the school budget are not being cut to support increased teacher wages. He found that "the mean level of the total operating tax rate for the sample of bargaining districts is $2.93 per $100 of 'equalized' assessed valuation compared to a tax rate of $2.69 in nonbargaining districts" (pp. 236-37). He concludes that the taxpayers are footing the bill for teacher salary increases. "The hypothesis that higher teacher compensation costs imposed by collective bargaining are funded through an expansion in the size or level of the total operating budget is supported" (p. 236).

Recent moves by voters to reduce taxes, led by Proposition 13 in California, have changed the entire complexion of educational finance in the United States. Cognizant of this trend, Gallagher is not willing to project his findings indefinitely into the future:

> It is conceivable that as school districts increase their operating tax rates and approach the legal allowable level of taxation as a result of collective bargaining activity and other nonbargaining factors such as declining levels of state aid, school officials may encounter increasing taxpayer resistance to continued budget expansion through taxation. As a result, future total teacher compensation gains generated from collective bargaining activity may influence school officials to pursue the alternative of internal budget reductions in nonteacher compensation areas as a method of funding teacher compensation expenditures (p. 237).

Gallagher's conclusions are challenged by Hall and Carroll (1973), who approach the question of increased costs from a different point of view and conclude that taxpayers are not pulling a heavier load after all. Hall and Carroll analyzed data from 118 elementary school districts in suburban Cook County, Illinois, for the school year 1968-69, with particular emphasis on the relationship between teachers' salaries and class size.

> Generally, our findings indicate that teachers' salaries are being increased by no more than $200 while the student-teacher ratio is being increased by about one. With a mean salary of $9,133 and an average of 21.3 students per teacher, average salary costs per pupil would appear to be approximately $430. It is doubtful whether the difference can be explained by any gains in fringe benefits which are not reflected in salary data. As long as teachers are willing to accept this arrangement, there would appear to be little cause for alarm among taxpayers over the rise of collective negotiations among public school faculties in their districts (p. 841).

Their finding of an apparent link between collective bargaining and a larger student-teacher ratio "lends support to the common allegation that school boards are offering teachers higher salaries in exchange for larger classes and that these offers are being accepted" (pp. 840-41). The significance to taxpayers of this finding should be clear.

Chambers (1978), too, considers the impact of increased funding for schools, whether it results from greater union bargaining or from school finance reform. He asks if more school funding would only "be used to increase teachers' salaries and would not be used to improve the quantity or quality of school personnel" (p. 155). In his study of a sample of California school districts, Chambers found that "for the hypothetical $100 increase in the school budgets, the lower spending districts allocate about 25% of the budget increment to reducing class sizes [a measure of increased quality] while allocating only 10% to increasing teachers' salaries" (p. 155). He asks further, Why shouldn't new dollars go into improving teachers' salaries? Would not the increases function not only to raise wages of teachers already working in the district but also "serve to attract better quality personnel at the margins" (p. 156)?

Chambers urges that his model of how funds are allocated in public schools be integrated into research on public-sector resource allocation. Although he does not directly address the role of unions in changing the allocation of resources, he does provide a useful model for understanding how the structure of public school funding operates.

Conclusion

The conflicting interpretations of Gallagher (1978), Chambers (1978), and Hall and Carroll (1973) seem to be a particularly fitting place to conclude this review. While researchers in this field can agree generally on the existence of a positive correlation between collective bargaining activity and increased teacher salary and nonsalary benefits, there is no consensus beyond this point. As is the case with much social science investigation, this research generates just as many new questions as it purports to answer.

Future research on finance and unionization should treat these questions:

1. Are the increased costs of collective bargaining (salaries and benefits) financed by cutting allocations to other program areas, by increasing taxes, or by upping class size?
2. Do unions progressively lose their effectiveness in obtaining financial gains?
3. Are teacher unions more (or less) effective than other public-sector unions?
4. Is there a relationship between a union's level of bargaining activity and its success in gaining financial benefits at the bargaining table?
5. What are the continuing impacts, if any, of bargaining, strikes, and their costs on educational quality in the United States?

Opportunity for Research

Much of the research reviewed in this essay on collective bargaining, striking, and their financial impact was performed prior to recent declines in student population, number of schools, staff size, and national support for school funding. An opportunity exists, then, to expand studies of educational labor relations in a constricting market. David Lewin (1977), in his retrospective analysis, makes three important comments in this regard: First, "It seems likely that labor scholars will be afforded the opportunity of testing their observations about governmental labor relations against the phenomenon of cyclical changes in the economy of the public sector" (p. 144).

Second, a renewed study of public-sector labor relations—important in its own right—is vital "also for the stimulus that it provides to the reexamination of private sector labor relations" (p. 144). Finally, Lewin takes a similar perspective to the one we have assumed in this essay: a comparative approach to public and private labor relations as a means of grasping both. He writes: "Integration of knowledge about public and private sector union-management relations would contribute substantially to a broader understanding of the contemporary American industrial relations system" (p. 144)—of which public education is a large and important part.

References

Alexander, Elliott. "Men in the Middle Seek Greater Value." *National Elementary Principal*, 51, 2 (October 1971), pp. 48-53.

Alluto, Joseph A., and Belasco, James A. "Determinants of Attitudinal Militancy among Teachers and Nurses." *Industrial and Labor Relations Review*, 27, 2 (January 1974), pp. 216-27.

American Federation of Teachers. *American Federation of Teachers Officers' Report to the AFT Convention*. Washington, D.C.: 1974.

Bain, George Sayers. *The Growth of White-Collar Unionism*. London: Oxford University Press, 1970.

Baird, Robert N., and Landon, John H. "The Effects of Collective Bargaining on Public School Teachers' Salaries: Comment." *Industrial and Labor Relations Review*, (April 1972), pp. 410-17.

Barrett, Jerome T., and Lobel, Ira B. "Public Sector Strikes—Legislative and Court Treatment." *Monthly Labor Review*, (September 1974), pp. 19-22.

Batchelder, Richard D. "Today's Militant Teachers." *Education Digest*, 31, 4 (December 1965), pp. 22-23.

Belasco, James A.; Alluto, Joseph A.; and Glassman, Alan. "A Case Study of Community and Teacher Expectations Concerning the Authority Structure of School Systems." *Education and Urban Society*, (November 1971), pp. 89-96.

Bernstein, I. "The Growth of American Unions, 1945-1960." *Labor History*, 2 (1961), p. 131.

Bernstein, I.; Enarson, H. L.; and Fleming, R. W., eds. *Emergency Disputes and National Policy*. New York: Harper and Row, 1955.

Billings, Richard M., and Greenya, John. *Power to the Public Worker*. Washington, D.C.: Robert B. Luca, Inc., 1974.

"The Brewing—and, Perhaps, Still Preventable—Revolt of the School Principals." *The American School Board Journal*, (January 1976), pp. 25-27.

Bridges, Edwin M. "Administrative Man: Origin or Pawn in Decision-Making." *Educational Administration Quarterly*, 6 (Winter 1970), pp. 7-25.

Bridges, Edwin M., and Cooper, Bruce S. "Collective Bargaining for Administrators." *Theory Into Practice*, 15 (October 1976), pp. 303-12.

Bruno, James E., and Nelken, Ira. "An Empirical Analysis on Propensity for Teachers to Strike." *Educational Administration Quarterly*, (Spring 1975), pp. 66-85.

Burton, John F. "The Extent of Collective Bargaining in the Public Sector." In *Public-Sector Bargaining*, edited by Benjamin Aaron, Joseph R. Grodin, and James C. Stern. Washington, D.C.: Industrial Relations Research Association, 1979.

Burton, John F., and Krider, Charles. "The Role and Consequence of Striking Public Employees." *The Yale Law Journal*, 79, 3 (January 1970), pp. 418-43.

Callahan, Raymond E. *Education and the Cult of Efficiency*. Chicago: University of Chicago Press, 1962.

Cassell, F., and Baron, J. "Ocean Hill-Brownsville: A Modern Greek Tragedy." Unpublished manuscript. n.p.: 1974.

Chamberlain, Neil W. *Social Responsibility and Strikes*. New York: Harper and Row, 1953.

Chamberlain, Neil W. "Comparability Pay and Compulsory Arbitration in Municipal Bargaining." Argument made to Public Employment Relations Board, reprinted in *Proceedings of 5th Annual Orvil Dreyfoos Conference*, Dartmouth College. See Case Number D 0003 PERB New York.

Chamberlain, Neil W., and Kuhn, James W. *Collective Bargaining*. 2d ed. New York: McGraw-Hill, 1965.

Chambers, Jay G. "An Analysis of Resource Allocation in Public School Districts." *Public Finance Quarterly*, 6, 2 (April 1978), pp. 131-60.

Cheng, Charles W. *Altering Collective Bargaining: Citizen Participation in Education Decision-Making*. New York: Praeger, 1976a.

Cheng, Charles W. "Community Participation in Teacher Collective Bargaining: Problems and Prospects." *Harvard Education Review*, 463 (1976b), pp. 153-74.

Cheng, Charles W.; Tamer, Irving; and Barron, Melanie. "A Framework for Citizen Involvement in Teacher Negotiations." *Education and Urban Society*, 11, 2 (February 1979), pp. 219-39.

Colton, David, L. "Injunctions and Teachers Strikes." *Administrator's Handbook*, (April 1975), pp. 1-4.

References

Colton, David L. "The Influence of an Anti-Strike Injunction." Paper presented at annual meeting of the American Educational Research Association, San Francisco, April 19-23, 1976.

Colton, David L. "Why, When and How School Boards Use Injunctions to Stifle Teacher Strikes." *The American School Board Journal*, (March 1977), pp. 32-35.

Commons, John Rogers. *Institutional Economics, Its Place in Political Economy*. New York: Macmillan, 1934.

Commons, John Rogers. *Legal Foundations of Capitalism*. Madison, Wisconsin: University of Wisconsin Press, 1957.

Cooper, Bruce S. "Middle Management Unionization in Education." *Administrator's Notebook*, (Spring 1975).

Cooper, Bruce S. "Collective Bargaining Comes to School Management." *Phi Delta Kappan*, (October 1976), pp. 202-4.

Cooper, Bruce S. "Federal Action and Collective Bargaining for Public Supervisors: Basis for an Argument." *Public Personnel Management*, 6, 5 (Fall 1978), pp. 341-52.

Cooper, Bruce S. "Collective Bargaining for School Administrators Four Years Later." *Phi Delta Kappan*, (October 1979), pp. 130-31.

Cooper, Bruce S., and Murrmann, Kent F. "Independent But Cooperative: The Near-Death of the 'Management Team' in New Jersey." *Educational Viewpoints*, (Spring 1981), pp. 4-18.

Cresswell, Anthony M., and Murphy, Michael J. *Education and Collective Bargaining: Readings in Policy and Research*. Berkeley, California: McCutchan Publishing Corporation, 1979.

Cresswell, Anthony M.; Murphy, Michael J.; and Kerchner, Charles T. *Teachers, Unions, and Collective Bargaining in Education*. Berkeley, California: McCutchan Publishing Corporation, 1980.

Daykin, Walter L. "The Status of Supervisory Employees under the National Labor Relations Act." *Yale Law Journal*, 55 (1945-46), pp. 754-77.

Dempsey, Richard A. "Negotiations: The Road Ahead." Paper presented at National Association of Secondary School Principals annual convention, 57th, Dallas, Texas, 1973.

Doering, Barbara. "Impasse Issues in Teacher Disputes Submitted to Factfinding in New York." *The Arbitration Journal*, 27, 1 (March, 1972), pp. 1-17.

Doherty, Robert E. "Public Education." In *Collective Bargaining: Contemporary American Experience*, pp. 487-552. Madison, Wisconsin: Industrial Relations Research Association, 1980.

Donley, Marshall O., Jr. *Power to the Teacher: How America's Educators Became Militant*. Bloomington, Indiana: Indiana University Press, 1976.

Druckman, D. "Dogmatism, Prenegotiation Experience, and Simulated Group Representation as Determinants of Dyadic Behavior in a Bargaining Situation." *Journal of Personality and Social Psychology*, 6 (1967), pp. 279-90.

Dubin, Robert, ed. *Human Relations in Administration*. New York: Prentice-Hall, 1955. (p. 159ff).

Duke, Daniel; Showers, Beverly K.; and Imber, Michael. "Costs to Teachers of Involvement in School Decision-Making." In mimeo. 1979.

Edelstein, J. David, and Warner, Malcolm. *Comparative Union Democracy*. New York: John Wiley, 1968.

Ehrenberg, Ronald. *An Economic Analysis of Local Government Employment and Wages*. Prepared for Department of Labor, December 1973.

Elam, Stanley M. "Collective Bargaining and Strikes or Professional Negotiations and Sanctions?" *The Education Digest*, (January 1963), pp. 1-4.

Elam, Stanley M. *A Decade of Gallup Polls of Attitudes toward Education: 1969-1978*. Bloomington, Indiana: Phi Delta Kappa, 1978.

Engel, Ross A. "Teacher Negotiation: History and Comment." *Journal of Law and Education*, (July 1972), pp. 487-95.

Erickson, Donald A. "Should the Nation's Schools Be Made to Compete?" *Phi Delta Kappan*, (September 1979), pp. 14-17, 77.

Fantini, M.; Gittell, M.; and Magat, R. *Community Control and the Urban School*. New York: Praeger, 1970.

Feldman, Sandra. *The Burden of Blame-Placing*. New York: United Federation of Teachers, 1969.

Feuille, Peter. "Selected Benefits and Costs of Compulsory Arbitration." *Industrial and Labor Relations Review*, 33, 1 (October 1979), pp. 64-76.

Fowler, Robert Booth. "Public Employees Strikes and Political Theory." In *Collective Bargaining in Government*, edited by J. J. Loewenberg and M. H. Moscoro, pp. 291-96. Englewood Cliffs, New Jersey: Prentice-Hall, 1973.

Frankfurter, Felix, and Greene, Nathan. *The Labor Injunction*. New York: Macmillan, 1930.

Frey, Donald E. "Wage Determination in Public Schools and the Effects of Unionization." In *Labor in the Public and Nonprofit Sectors*, edited by Daniel S. Hamermesh, pp. 183-219. Princeton, New Jersey: Princeton University Press, 1975.

Friedman, D. D. "An Analytical Study of Strikes by Public School Teachers in the United States." Unpublished dissertation, Columbia University, 1966.

Gallagher, Daniel G. "Teacher Bargaining and School District Expenditures." *Industrial Relations*, (May 1978), pp. 231-37.

Getman, J. G.; Goldberg, S. B.; and Herman, J. B. *Union Representation Election: Law and Reality.* New York: Russell Sage, 1976.

Goldbloom, Maurice J. "The New York School Crisis." In *Schools in Crisis.* New York: Popular Library, 1969.

Governor's Committee on Public Employee Relations. *Final Report.* Albany: State of New York, 1966.

Grodin, Joseph. "Political Aspects of Public Sector Interest Arbitration." *Industrial Relations Law Journal,* 33, 1 (March 1976), pp. 20-31.

Gross, Neal, and Herriott, Robert E. *Staff Leadership in Public Schools: A Sociological Analysis.* New York: John Wiley and Sons, 1965.

Guinan, Matthew. "The Unreal Distinction between Public and Private Sectors." *Monthly Labor Review,* (September 1973), pp. 46-47.

Gustman, Alan L., and Segal, Martin. *The Impact of Teachers' Unions.* National Institute of Education, Project Number 4-0136, September, 1976.

Gustman, Alan L., and Segal, Martin. "Interstate Variations in Teachers' Pensions." *Industrial Relations,* 16, 3 (October 1977), pp. 335-44.

Hall, W. Clayton, and Carroll, Norman E. "The Effect of Teachers' Organizations on Salaries and Class Size." *Industrial and Labor Relations Review,* (January 1973), pp. 834-41.

Hamner, W. Clay, and Smith, Frank T. "Work Attitudes as Predictors of Unionization Activity." *Journal of Applied Psychology,* 63, 4 (1978), pp. 415-21.

"Hear This: Schools, Not Teachers Unions, Are in Charge of Schools: Who Says So? The U. S. Supreme Court, That's Who." *The American School Board Journal,* (August 1976), pp. 39-41.

Heddinger, Fred M. "Do Your Principals Have Enough Decision-Making Power? In Pennsylvania, They Do." *The American School Board Journal,* (February 1978), pp. 30-31.

Heller, Robert W. "The Principal's Role in Planning for a Teacher Strike." *NASSP Bulletin,* (May 1978), pp. 98-105.

Hemphill, John D.; Griffiths, Daniel E.; and Frederiksen, Norman. *Performance and Personality.* New York: Teachers College Press, 1962.

Herman, J. B. "Are Situational Contingencies Limiting Job Attitude-Job Performance Relationship?" *Organizational Behavior and Human Performances,* Volume 10. 1973. (pp. 208-224).

Herndon, T. *NEA Reporter,* April 1976.

Hetenyi, Laszlo. "Unionism in Education: The Ethics of It." *Educational Theory,* 28, 2 (Spring 1978), pp. 90-95.

Hirsch, Barry T. "Determinants of Unionization: An Analysis of Interarea Differences." *Industrial Labor Relations Review,* 33, 2 (January 1979), pp. 147-61.

Holmes, Alexander B. "Union Activity and Teacher Salary Structure." *Industrial Relations,* (Winter 1979).

Hopkins, Anne H.; Rawson, George E.; and Smith, Russell L. "The Impact of Public Employee Unionization on the Work Situation." Paper presented at the American Political Science Association annual meeting, September 2-5, 1975, San Francisco.

Hutchison, William I. "The Principal's Role during a Strike." *National Association of Secondary School Principals (NASSP) Bulletin*, (May 1971), pp. 172-84.

Irwin, James R. "Preparing for a Strike and Living with It After It Happens." Speech delivered at meeting of National Association of Secondary School Principals, New Orleans, Louisiana, January 15 and 17, 1977.

Isaacs, Charles S. "A Junior High School Teacher Tells It Like He Sees It." *The New York Times Magazine*, November 24, 1968, pp. 1, 52.

"It's Late, But There's Still Time to Give Your Principals a Real Say in Management." *The American School Board Journal*, (February 1976), pp. 32-34.

Johnson, Douglas F., and Pruitt, Dean G. "Preintervention Effects of Mediation versus Arbitration." *Journal of Applied Psychology*, 56, 1 (1972), pp. 1-10.

Kasper, Hirschel. "The Effects of Collective Bargaining on Public School Teachers' Salaries." *Industrial and Labor Relations Review*, (October 1970), pp. 57-72.

Kasper, Hirschel. "Reply." *Industrial and Labor Relations Review*, 25 (April 1973), pp. 417-23.

Katz, Michael B. *Class, Bureaucracy and Schools*. New York: Praeger, 1968.

Keough, William F., Jr. "Fence Mending after the Strike." Presentation at 1974 annual meeting of American Association of School Administrators.

Kerchner, Charles T. "Bargaining Costs in Public Schools: A Preliminary Assessment." *California Public Employee Relations*, (June 1979), pp. 16-25.

Kerchner, Charles T. *The Impact of Citizen Participation on Collective Bargaining and School Governance*. Study in progress, commissioned by National Institute of Education, Washington, D.C., 1980.

Kheel, T. W. "Resolving Deadlocks without Banning Strikes." *Monthly Labor Review*, 92 (July 1969), pp. 62-63.

Kilberg, William J. "A Limited Right to Strike for Public Employees." *Harvard Journal on Legislation*, November 1969.

Knight, Frank H. *Freedom and Reform*. New York: Harper and Row, 1947.

Kochan, Thomas A. "Correlates of State Public Employment Bargaining Laws." *Industrial Relations*, 12, 3 (October 1973), pp. 322-37.

Krauschaar, Otto. *American Nonpublic Schools: Patterns in Diversity*. Baltimore: Johns Hopkins University Press, 1968.

Larrowe, Charles P. "A Meteor on the Industrial Relations Horizon: The Foreman's Association of America." *Labor History*, 2, 3 (Fall 1961), pp. 259-93.

Leiserson, William M. "Constitutional Government in American Industries." *American Economic Review*, Volume 12, Supplement, 1922.

Lewin, David. "Public Sector Labor Relations." *Labor History*, 18, 1 (Winter 1977), pp. 134-44.

Lieberman, Myron. "It's an Invitation to Trouble." *The American School Board Journal*, (June 1977), pp. 25-27.

Lieberman, Myron, and Moskow, Michael H. *Collective Negotiations for Teachers*. Chicago: Rand McNally, 1966.

Lipsky, David B., and Drotning, John E. "The Influence of Collective Bargaining on Teachers' Salaries in New York State." *Industrial and Labor Relations Review*, (October 1973), pp. 18-35.

Lockwood, David. *The Blackcoated Worker*. London: Allen and Unwin, 1958.

Loewenberg, J. Joseph. "Compulsory Arbitration for Police and Fire Fighters in Pennsylvania in 1968." *Industrial and Labor Relations Review*, 23, 3 (April 1970), pp. 309-19.

Loewenberg, J. Joseph, and Moskow, Michael H. *Collective Bargaining in Government*. Englewood Cliffs, New Jersey: Prentice-Hall, 1972.

Lortie, Dan C. "Control and Autonomy of Elementary School Teachers." In *The Semi-Professions*, edited by A. Etzioni. Glencoe, Illinois: The Free Press. 1969.

Lortie, Dan C. *Schoolteacher: A Sociological Study*. Chicago: University of Chicago Press, 1977.

Lubetsky, Kenneth P. "Will the NEA and the AFT Ever Merge?" *The Education Forum*, (March 1977), pp. 309-16.

Mann, Floyd C., and Dent, James K. "The Supervisor: Member of Two Organizational Families." *Harvard Business Review*, 32, 6 (December 1954), pp. 103-12.

Martin, James E. "State Employee Affiliation and Attitude Differences." *Journal of Applied Psychology*, 65, 5 (1978), pp. 654-57.

Mayer, Martin. *The Teachers Strike*. New York: Harper and Row, 1969.

McAvoy, Joan Zeldon. "Binding Arbitration on Contract Terms: A New Approach to the Resolution of Disputes in the Public Sector." *Columbia Law Review*, 72 (1972), pp. 1192-1213.

McDonnell, Lorraine, and Anthony, Pascal. *Organized Teachers in American Schools*. Santa Monica, California: Rand Corporation, 1979.

McGinley, Daniel J., and Rafferty, Bernard F. "It's Working in Philadelphia." *The Elementary Principal*, 53, 1 (November-December 1973), pp. 25-28.

McKelvey, Jean T. "Factfinding in Public Employment Disputes: Promise or Illusion?" *Industrial and Labor Relations Review*, 22, 4 (July 1969).

Metzler, John H. "Management's Losing Struggle against Union Organization." *Personnel Administration*, 24, 1 (January-February 1961), pp. 27-30.

Mitchell, Donald. *Leadership in Public Education Study.* Washington, D.C.: Academy for Educational Development, Inc., 1972.

Moore, William J. "An Analysis of Teacher Union Growth." *Industrial Relations*, 17, 2 (May 1978), pp. 204-15.

Moskow, Michael H.; Loewenberg, J. Joseph; and Koziara, Edward C. *Collective Bargaining in Public Employment.* New York: Random House, 1970.

Murphy, Michael J. "Teachers Strikes: A Social-Psychological Analysis." Unpublished dissertation, Claremont Graduate School, 1971.

Nasstrom, Roy R., and Brelsford, Robert L. "Some Characteristics of Militant Teachers: A Reassessment Based on an Indiana Study." *Journal of Collective Bargaining*, 5, 3 (1976), pp. 247-56.

National Center for Education Statistics. 1976, pp. 7, 20-22.

National Coalition for Teacher Unity. "Teacher-Unity." Washington, D.C., 1974.

National Education Association. *Proceedings.* Washington, D.C.: 1962.

National Education Association. *Press Release.* 117th Annual Meeting, Detroit, Michigan, June 30-July 5, 1979.

National School Boards Association. *Collective Bargaining—Practices and Attitudes of School Management.* Research Report 1977-2. Washington, D.C.: 1977.

Neal, Richard G. *Avoiding and Controlling Teacher Strikes.* Washington, D.C.: Educational Service Bureau, Incorporated, 1971.

Neilsen, John, and Shanker, Albert. "Time to End Organizational Rivalries." *American Teacher*, 63 (March 1979), p. 9.

Nolte, M. Chester. *Status and Scope of Collective Bargaining in Public Education.* Eugene: The ERIC Clearinghouse on Educational Administration, University of Oregon, 1970.

Northrup, Herbert R. *Compulsory Arbitration and Government Intervention in Labor Disputes.* Washington, D.C.: Labor Policy Association, Incorporated, 1966.

O'Callaghan, Mike. "Nevada's Binding Factfinding Law: A Viable Alternative?" *State Government*, 49, 4 (Autumn 1976), pp. 268-72.

O'Connell, James P., and Heller, Robert W. "Factors Leading to Impasse in Teacher/School Board Collective Bargaining." Paper presented at the annual meeting of the American Educational Research Association, April 19-23, 1976.

Ohio Association of Elementary School Principals. *The Administrative Team.* Westerville, Ohio: Ohio Association of Elementary Principals, 1971.

Olson, Mancur. *The Logic of Collective Action: Public Goods and the Theory of Groups*. Cambridge, Massachusetts: Harvard University Press, 1971. (Chapter 3).

Ostroff, Betty S. "The Metamorphosis of a Professional Association into a Union." Unpublished dissertation, Teachers College, Columbus University, 1974.

Pegnetter, Richard. "Fact Finding and Teacher Salary Disputes." *Industrial and Labor Relations Review*, 24, 2 (January 1971).

Perry, Charles R. "Teacher Bargaining: The Experience in Nine Systems." *Industrial and Labor Relations Review*, 33, 1 (October 1979), pp. 3-17.

Perry, Charles R., and Wildman, Wesley A. *The Impact of Negotiations in Public Education: The Evidence from the Schools*. Worthington, Ohio: Charles A. Jones Co., 1970.

Perry, James R. "Public Policy and Public Employee Strikes." *Industrial Relations*, 16, 3 (October 1977), pp. 273-82.

Phelps, Orme W. "Compulsory Arbitration: Some Perspectives." *Industrial and Labor Relations Review*, 18, 1 (October 1964), pp. 81-91.

Phillips, William M., Jr., and Conforti, Joseph M. "Social Conflict: Teachers Strikes in Newark, 1964-1971: An Issue Paper on a Topical Subject in Education." Trenton, New Jersey: New Jersey Department of Education, October 1972.

Pierce, Paul Revere. *The Origin and Development of the Public School Principalship*. Chicago: University of Chicago, 1935.

Pierson, Frank. "An Evaluation of Emergency Provisions." In *Emergency Disputes and National Policy*, edited by I. Bernstein, H. L. Enarson, and R. W. Fleming, pp. 132-38. New York: Harper and Row, 1955.

Prosten, Richard. "Discussion." *IRRA 30th Annual Proceedings*, 1978, p. 446.

Rains, Harry H. "Compulsory Arbitration and the Public Interest: Redefining the Arbitrator's Responsibilities." *Employee Relations Law Journal*, (Spring 1976), pp. 643-47.

Ravitch, Diane. *The Great School Wars, New York City, 1805-1973*. New York: Basic Books, 1974.

Rehmus, Charles M. "Public Management and Collective Negotiations." In *Collective Negotiations and Educational Administration*, edited by Roy B. Allen and John Schmid, pp. 61-72. Columbus, Ohio: University Council for Educational Administration, no date.

Rehmus, Charles M., and Wilner, Evan. *The Economic Results of Teacher Bargaining: Michigan's First Two Years*. Ann Arbor: Institute of Labor and Industrial Relations, 1965.

Roethlisberger, Fritz J. "The Foreman: Master and Victim of Double Talk." *Harvard Business Review*, (1945), pp. 279-84.

Rogers, David. *110 Livingston Street*. New York: Vintage, 1968.

Roomkin, Myron. "Union Structure, Internal Control, and Strike Activity." *Industrial and Labor Relations Review*, (1972), pp. 198-214.

Ross, Arthur M., and Hartman, Paul T. *Changing Patterns of Industrial Conflict*. New York: John Wiley and Sons, 1960.

Rynecki, Steven, and Gausden, Thomas. "Current Trends in Public Sector Impasse Resolution." *State Government*, 49, 4 (Autumn 1976), pp. 273-76.

Sallot, Jeff. "Turn This School Board's Nine Hard Lessons from a Teacher Strike into Easy Lessons for Your Own Board." *The American School Board Journal*, (June 1977), pp. 35-36.

Sally, Columbus; McPherson, R. Bruce; and Baehr, Melany E. "What Principals Do: A Preliminary Occupational Analysis." In *The Principal in Metropolitan Schools*, edited by Donald A. Erickson and Theodore L. Reller, pp. 22-39. Berkeley, California: McCutchan, 1979.

Salmon, Paul B. "Are the Administrative Team and Collective Bargaining Compatible?" *Compact*, 12 (June 1972), pp. 1-8.

Sarason, S. C.; Cheng, C.; Cowden, P.; Davies, D.; Lorentz, E.; Maton, K.; and Reppucci, N. *The Community at the Bargaining Table*. Boston: Institute for Basic Education, 1975.

Schmenner, R.W. "The Determinants of Municipal Employee Wages." *Review of Economics and Statistics*, 55 (February 1973), pp. 83-90.

Schofield, Dee. *Collective Negotiations and the Principal*. Arlington, Virginia; and Eugene, Oregon: National Association of Elementary School Principals; and ERIC Clearinghouse on Educational Management, University of Oregon, 1976.

Seay, Maurice F. "Administrative Acts and Their Consequences." In *Urban Schooling*, edited by Herbert C. Rudman and Richard L. Featherstone. New York: Harcourt, Brace & World, 1968.

Seidman, Joel; London, Jack; Karsh, Bernard; and Tagliacozzo, Daisy L. *The Worker Views His Union*. Chicago: University of Chicago Press, 1958.

Shanker, Albert L. "Why Teachers Need the Right to Strike." *Monthly Labor Review*, 99 (1973), pp. 48-51.

Shapiro, David. "Relative Wage Effects of Unions in the Public and Private Sectors." *Industrial and Labor Relations Review*, January 1978, pp. 193-203.

Shevis, James M. "Twenty-Four Unions Establish Public Employee Department." *AFL-CIO News*, (1974), p. 1.

Shils, Edward S., and Whittier, C. Taylor. *Teachers, Administrators, and Collective Bargaining*. New York: Thomas Y. Crowell Company, 1968.

Sinclair, John E. "Separate Bargaining Units for Principals—The Wrong Solution." *NASSP Bulletin*, (May 1977), pp. 52-56.

Siskind, David. *One Thousand Strikes of Government Employees*. New York: Columbia University Press, 1940, pp. 232, 258-59.

Slichter, Sumner. *Union Policies and Industrial Management*. Washington, D.C.: The Brookings Institution, 1941.

Smith, F. J. "Work Attitudes as Predictors of Attendance on a Specific Day." *Journal of Applied Psychology*, 62 (1977), pp. 16-19.

Spero, Sterling D. *Government as Employer*. New York: Remsen Press, 1948.

Staudohar, Paul D. "The Grievance Arbitration and No-Strike Model in Public Employment." *Arbitration Journal*, (June 1976), pp. 116-24.

Steele, Helen H. "A Teacher's View." *Phi Delta Kappan*, (May 1976), pp. 590-92.

Stern, James L.; Rehmus, Charles M.; Loewenberg, J. Joseph; Hirschel, Kasper; and Dennis, Barbara D. *Final Offer Arbitration*. Lexington, Massachusetts: Lexington Books, 1975.

Stevens, Carl M. "Is Compulsory Arbitration Compatible with Bargaining?" *Industrial Relations*, 5, 2 (February 1966), pp. 38-52.

Stieber, Jack. "A New Approach to Strikes in Public Employment." *MSU Business Topics*, (Autumn 1967), pp. 67-71.

Stinnett, T. M. *Turmoil in Teaching*. New York: Macmillan Company, 1968.

Strom, David. "Teacher Unionism: An Assessment." *Education and Urban Society*, 11, 2 (February 1979), pp. 152-67.

Sturmthal, Adolf, ed. *White-Collar Trade Unions: Contemporary Developments in Industrialized Societies*. Urbana, Illinois: University of Illinois Press, 1966.

Tannenbaum, Arnold S. "Unions." In *Handbook of Organizations*, edited by James G. March, pp. 710-63. Chicago: Rand McNally, 1965.

Thornton, Robert J. "The Effects of Collective Negotiations on Teachers' Salaries." *Quarterly Review of Economics and Business*, (1970), pp. 37-46.

Torrence, William D. "And What Do Teachers Strike Most Over? Wages, Of Course." *American School Board Journal*, (March 1976), p. 24.

Tyack, David B. *The One Best System*. Cambridge, Massachusetts: Harvard University Press, 1970.

Ulman, Lloyd. *The Rise of the National Union*. Cambridge, Massachusetts: Harvard University Press, 1968.

U. S. Bureau of the Census. *Labor-Management Relations in State and Local Government: 1976*. Washington, D.C.: U. S. Government Printing Office, Series GSS Number 88, 1975, p. 5.

Vagts, Christopher, and Stone, Robert B. *Anatomy of a Teacher Strike*. West Nyack, New York: Parker Publishing Company, 1969.

Van de Vall. *Labor Organizations*. Cambridge: Cambridge University Press, 1970.

Vogel, Alfred. "Your Clerical Workers are Ripe for Unionism." *Harvard Business Review*, (March/April 1971), pp. 48-54.

Wagstaff, Connie H. "Unionized Principals. You May Be Next." *NASSP Bulletin*, (November 1973), pp. 40-47.

Walker, Charles R.; Guest, Robert H.; and Turner, Arthur N. *The Foreman on the Assembly Line*. Cambridge, Massachusetts: Harvard University Press, 1956.

Warner, Kenneth S.; Chisholm, Rupert F.; and Munzenrider, Robert F. "Motives for Unionization among State Social Service Employees." *Public Personnel Management*, (May-June 1978), pp. 181-90.

Wasserman, Miriam. *The School Fix, NYC, USA*. New York: Simon and Schuster, 1970.

Watson, Bernard. "The Principal Against the System." In *The Principal in Metropolitan Schools*, edited by D. A. Erickson and R. L. Reller, pp. 40-54. Berkeley, California: McCutchan Publishing Corporation, 1979.

Wellington, Harry H., and Winter, Ralph K. "The Limits of Collective Bargaining in Public Employment." *The Yale Law Journal*, 77, 7 (June 1969).

Wellington, Harry H., and Winter, Ralph K. "More on Strikes by Public Employees." *Yale Law Review*, 79 (1970), pp. 441-43.

"When Teachers Go Out on Strike." *National Elementary Principal*, (March/April 1977), pp. 49-53.

White, Sheila C. "Work Stoppages of Government Employees." *Monthly Labor Review*, (December 1969), pp. 61-69.

Wildman, W. A. "Collective Action by Public School Teachers." *Industrial and Labor Relations Review*, (October 1964), pp. 3-19.

Wilson, Peter. "The Impact of Public Sector Labor Relations on the Private Sector." *The Personnel Administrator*, (June 1977), pp. 20-23, 50.

Winston, Sheldon. "The Addendum to Your District's Strike Plan." *Thrust for Educational Leadership*, (November 1975), pp. 22-24.

Wollett, D. H. "The Taylor Law and the Strike Ban." Paper presented to the Association of Labor Mediation Agencies, Puerto Rico, August 20, 1968. Published in BNA, *Public Employer Organization and Bargaining*, chapter 4, p. 30.

Wood, C. "Reds and Lost Wages." In *One Thousand Strikes of Government Employees*, by D. Siskind. New York: Arno Press, 1971. (Reproduction of 1970 edition).

Wray, D. E. "Marginal Men of Industry: The Foremen." *American Journal of Sociology*, (January 1949), pp. 290-99.

Yaffe, B., and Goldblatt, H. *Factfinding in Public Employment Disputes in New York State: More Promise than Illusion*. Ithaca: New York State School of Industrial and Labor Relations, 1971.

Yerkovich, Raymond J. "Teacher Militancy: An Analysis of Human Need." *The Clearinghouse*, 41, 8 (April 1967), pp. 458-61.